Amadeu Rossi

The Language of Emotions
A Complete Guide to Emotional Management

Original title: A Linguagem das Emoções

Copyright © 2024, published by Luiz Antonio dos Santos ME.

This book is a non-fiction work that explores practices and concepts in the field of emotional intelligence and feelings management. Through a comprehensive approach, the author offers practical tools to understand emotions, promote emotional balance, and cultivate resilience.

1st Edition
Production Team

Author: Amadeu Rossi
Editor: Luiz Santos
Revision: Robson Sass
Cover: Studios Booklas / Claudio Ambrásio
Layout: Regis Bennet
Translation: Emily Reis
Publication and Identification
The Language of Emotions
Publisher: Booklas, 2024
Categories: Psychology / Personal Development / Emotional Management

DDC: 152.4 - CDU: 159.942
All rights reserved to:
Luiz Antonio dos Santos ME / Booklas

No part of this book may be reproduced, stored in a retrieval system, or transmitted by any means - electronic, mechanical, photocopying, recording, or otherwise - without 1 the prior and express permission of the copyright 2 holder.

Summary

Prologue 6
Chapter 1 Introduction 8
Chapter 2 Self-knowledge... 12
Chapter 3 Emotional Intelligence 16
Chapter 4 Physiology of Emotions 20
Chapter 5 Thoughts and Emotions............................... 24
Chapter 6 The Language of Emotions 28
Chapter 7 External Influences..................................... 32
Chapter 8 Positive Emotions....................................... 36
Chapter 9 Negative Emotions 40
Chapter 10 Emotional Resilience................................. 44
Chapter 11 Self-Observation....................................... 48
Chapter 12 Mindfulness 52
Chapter 13 Conscious Breathing................................. 56
Chapter 14 Relaxation... 60
Chapter 15 Meditation 63
Chapter 16 Nonviolent Communication 67
Chapter 17 Assertiveness 71
Chapter 18 Managing Stress 75
Chapter 19 Dealing with Anger 79
Chapter 20 Overcoming Sadness 83
Chapter 21 Overcoming Fear 87
Chapter 22 Self-Compassion 91
Chapter 23 Forgiveness... 94

Chapter 24 Gratitude 97
Chapter 25 Positive Thinking 101
Chapter 26 Emotional Management in Relationships............... 106
Chapter 27 Emotional Management in the Family 109
Chapter 28 Emotional Management at Work 113
Chapter 29 Emotional Management in Education 117
Chapter 30 Emotional Management and Mental Health............ 121
Chapter 31 Self-Esteem 125
Chapter 32 Confidence: Developing Inner Strength................ 129
Chapter 33 Motivation: Awakening the Inner Strength........... 133
Chapter 34 Creativity: Awakening the Imaginative Potential .. 137
Chapter 35 Spirituality and Emotional Management................. 141
Chapter 36 Body and Mind: The Dance of Well-being 145
Chapter 37 Food and Emotions: 149
Chapter 38 Physical Exercise and Emotions: 153
Chapter 39 Sleep and Emotions: The Symphony of Rest......... 157
Chapter 40 Technology and Emotions....................................... 161
Chapter 41 The Art of Adaptation 165
Chapter 42 The Compass of Emotional Intelligence 169
Chapter 43 Aligning Emotions with Goals 173
Chapter 44 Overcoming Trauma.. 178
Chapter 45 Dealing with Loss.. 182
Chapter 46 Acceptance: Embracing Reality with Serenity...... 186
Chapter 47 Exploring the Depths of the Psyche 190
Chapter 48 Social Intelligence 194
Chapter 49 Leadership and Emotional Management................. 198
Chapter 50 Emotional Management in the Modern World....... 202

Chapter 51 Emotional Management in Practice 206
Chapter 52 Creating an Action Plan 210
Chapter 53 Expanding your Emotional Management Toolkit .. 214
Chapter 54 Maintaining Balance 218
Chapter 55 Reaping the Fruits of Emotional Management 222
Epilogue 225

Prologue

Dear reader,

Allow me to present this book to you not just as an editor, but as a fellow traveler. In my hands, it has revealed itself as a detailed map for navigating the turbulent seas of emotions, an essential guide for those seeking serenity amidst the chaos of the modern world.

If you feel overwhelmed by anxiety, lost in a whirlwind of feelings, or simply wish to deepen your connection with yourself, this book is for you.

The pages you are about to unveil offer a refuge, a space of welcome and learning. They will lead you on a transformative journey of self-discovery, revealing the strength and wisdom that reside within you.

This book is a balm for the soul, an invitation to healing and personal growth. I recommend it to all who wish to:

Master the art of emotional intelligence: understand and manage your emotions with mastery.

Cultivate resilience: strengthen yourself in the face of life's challenges and adversities.

Build healthier relationships: communicate with clarity and empathy, deepening your emotional bonds.

Find inner peace: calm the mind, quiet the heart and live with more serenity.

I trust that this work will touch you deeply, as it has touched me. May it be your beacon amidst the

storm, guiding you towards a fuller and more meaningful life.
    Luiz Santos
    Editor

Chapter 1
Introduction

Life can be understood as a rich tapestry of experiences, where each thread is represented by an emotion essential to our growth and understanding of ourselves. These threads intertwine in a unique design, formed by the experiences we accumulate over time. Joy, sadness, love, fear, and so many other emotions not only influence our decisions but also shape our worldview and our relationships. Therefore, mastering these emotions is more than a skill; it is a fundamental step in cultivating balance and wisdom in our journey. Emotional management, in this sense, is not just a necessity, but a powerful tool for living fully and consciously.

Emotions, when understood and managed properly, cease to be mere involuntary reflexes and become valuable allies. Each carries a purpose and a message about what we need to observe or transform. Thus, learning to interpret and use them intelligently does not mean ignoring them, but integrating them harmoniously into our routine. This process allows us to act more consciously, even in the face of challenges or adverse situations, and enables us to face life with resilience and confidence.

Throughout this book, you will be guided to explore and develop the ability to manage your emotions with greater clarity and purpose. This journey will provide not only a deeper understanding of yourself, but also practical tools to improve your relationships, make more assertive decisions, and live authentically. It is an invitation to access and awaken your inner potential, transforming emotions previously seen as obstacles into forces that drive your personal growth.

However, we often find ourselves adrift in this emotional sea, without the knowledge or tools necessary to deal with the turbulent waves that come our way. We feel overwhelmed by anger, paralyzed by fear, drowned by sadness, or lost in a whirlwind of anxiety. Emotions, which should be compasses to guide our lives, become storms that take us off course.

It is in this context that emotional management emerges as a beacon, illuminating the path to a more balanced, full, and meaningful life. Emotional management is the art of understanding, regulating, and using emotions intelligently and constructively. It is the ability to recognize and name one's own emotions, identify their triggers, and develop effective strategies to deal with them in a healthy way.

Mastering the art of emotional management is like acquiring an internal compass, which allows us to navigate life's challenges more safely. It is learning to transform emotions from enemies into allies, using their energy to drive personal growth, strengthen relationships, and achieve our goals.

Emotional management is not about suppressing or denying emotions. On the contrary, it is about welcoming them, understanding them, and integrating them into our life experience. It is about recognizing that all emotions, whether pleasant or unpleasant, have a purpose and can teach us something valuable about ourselves and the world around us.

By developing the ability to manage our emotions, we open doors to a more authentic and fulfilling life. We increase our resilience, improve our relationships, make more conscious decisions, and cultivate greater mental and physical well-being.

In this book, we will embark on a profound and transformative journey through the universe of emotional management. We will explore the fundamentals of emotional intelligence, unravel the connection between thoughts, emotions, and behaviors, and learn practical techniques for dealing with challenging emotions and cultivating positive ones.

We will learn to listen to the language of our body, identify emotional triggers, and develop effective strategies to regulate our responses. We will address the importance of self-compassion, forgiveness, and gratitude in building an emotionally balanced life.

I invite you to join me on this journey of self-discovery and transformation. Throughout the chapters, we will explore together the paths of emotional management, acquiring tools and knowledge that will empower you to create a fuller, more authentic, and meaningful life.

This book is an invitation to awaken the inner master who resides within you, the one who knows the wisdom of emotions and how to use them to create a happier, more balanced, and fulfilling life. It is a guide to freeing yourself from the shackles of uncontrolled emotions and navigating the waters of life with mastery.

Chapter 2
Self-knowledge

Self-knowledge is the essential foundation for a more conscious and fulfilling life, allowing you to deeply understand who you are and how you function in different contexts. It is a journey of introspection that goes beyond mere superficial reflections, seeking to identify thought patterns, predominant emotions, and the beliefs that shape your daily choices. This process is not only transformative but necessary to strengthen the connection with yourself and promote balance between mind, body, and emotions. Thus, by exploring your most intimate traits, you can develop a clear understanding of the internal dynamics that influence the way you live and interact with the world around you.

Paying attention to your reactions to everyday challenges reveals a lot about your motivations and limitations. This requires courage to face the complexity of your emotions and acknowledge aspects that are not always comfortable to admit. Accepting this duality - virtues and flaws - is what will allow you to grow, transforming difficulties into learning opportunities. When you acquire this understanding of yourself, you become able to align your actions with your most genuine values, building a path of greater authenticity and fulfillment.

Self-knowledge is not a fixed destination, but a continuous process that demands dedication and practice. Each discovery about yourself opens new doors for positive change, strengthening your ability to make decisions with more clarity and purpose. With a clear vision of who you are and what really matters, choices become more conscious, and results more meaningful. It is through this immersion in your essence that you find the freedom to live with more presence, balance and fullness, transforming yourself and your impact on the world around you.

Just as a navigator needs to know the stars to orient himself at sea, you need to know yourself to navigate safely through the waters of life. Self-knowledge is the inner compass that allows you to chart routes, avoid pitfalls and achieve your goals with more clarity and purpose.

The journey of self-knowledge is a fascinating adventure, full of discoveries and challenges. It is a continuous process of learning and growth, which requires courage to confront your shadows and humility to recognize your virtues.

To begin this journey, it is essential to cultivate self-observation. Pay attention to your thoughts, feelings and behaviors. Observe how you react in different situations, what your emotional triggers are and how your emotions influence your decisions.

Investigate your values and beliefs. What is really important to you? What are your principles? What are the beliefs that shape your worldview? Understanding your values is fundamental to making decisions aligned with your essence and living an authentic life.

Explore your motivations. What drives you? What are your dreams and aspirations? What makes you feel alive and fulfilled? Connecting with your motivations is like lighting an inner flame, which will propel you towards your goals.

Recognize your strengths and weaknesses. We all have qualities and skills that make us stand out, as well as areas that need to be developed. Identifying your strengths is essential to using your talents to your advantage. Recognizing your weaknesses is the first step to overcoming them and growing.

Accept your imperfections. The journey of self-knowledge is not about seeking perfection, but about embracing your humanity in its entirety. Recognize that you are a constantly evolving being, with qualities and flaws, lights and shadows. Embrace your authenticity and free yourself from the pressure to be perfect.

By knowing yourself deeply, you will be building a solid foundation for emotional management. You will better understand your reactions, identify your behavior patterns and develop more effective strategies to deal with your emotions.

By embracing self-knowledge, you begin to cultivate a more intimate relationship with yourself, where understanding and acceptance replace harsh judgments. This process strengthens your resilience and allows you to face challenges with more serenity and confidence. It is in the constant practice of observing and reflecting that you discover a transformative power: that of shaping your reality from more conscious choices aligned with your true essence.

As you progress on this journey, you will realize that self-knowledge not only enhances your relationship with yourself, but also enriches your connections with others. Clarity about your values, motivations and limits creates a solid foundation for more authentic and empathetic interactions. This authenticity, in turn, reverberates in your actions and decisions, consolidating a more integral and meaningful life.

The search for self-knowledge is, above all, an act of courage and self-love. It is a journey that demands patience and dedication, but offers as a reward a lighter and more harmonious existence. By looking inward, you find the keys to living more presently, with a clearer purpose and an unshakeable confidence in the path you have chosen to follow.

Chapter 3
Emotional Intelligence

Emotional intelligence is the competence that allows us to understand, manage and use our emotions in a conscious and constructive way, acting as a fundamental pillar for well-being and success in various aspects of life. It is this ability that transforms emotions into tools for self-development, allowing us to build healthy relationships, make sound decisions and overcome challenges with resilience and confidence. With it, we become able to identify the nuances of our feelings and interpret the emotions of others, creating fertile ground for empathy and cooperation.

Throughout life, emotional intelligence is revealed as an essential element in the journey of personal growth, equaling technical skills and intellectual knowledge. It presents itself not only as a guide for our daily interactions, but also as a lens through which we can see our motivations and respond to external stimuli in a balanced and conscious way. Mastering this competence means being prepared to deal with adverse situations, react calmly in times of crisis and transform conflicts into opportunities for learning and reconciliation.

Furthermore, the continuous practice of self-knowledge and emotional management allows us to cultivate a sense of purpose and direction in our lives. Emotional intelligence is not just an abstract concept or a theoretical idea, but a practical skill that enables us to navigate wisely through the challenges and rewards of human relationships. By developing it, we expand our capacity to connect with others, to align our personal goals with collective values and to create a positive and lasting impact on our surroundings.

Imagine emotional intelligence as an orchestra, composed of different instruments that, when played in harmony, produce an inspiring melody. Each instrument represents an essential skill of emotional intelligence, and the conductor is our consciousness, leading each element to create a symphony of well-being.

The pillars of emotional intelligence:

Self-awareness: It is the foundation of emotional intelligence. Just as a builder needs to know the terrain before building a house, we need to know our emotions, triggers and behavior patterns to build an emotionally solid life.

Self-control: It is the ability to regulate one's own emotions, preventing them from dominating us. It is like a helmsman who guides the ship through the storm, maintaining control even in challenging situations.

Self-motivation: It is the inner strength that drives us towards our goals, even in the face of obstacles. It is like an engine that moves us, fueling our persistence and enthusiasm.

Empathy: It is the ability to put yourself in another's shoes, understanding their emotions and perspectives. It is like a bridge that connects hearts, allowing us to build deeper and more meaningful relationships.

Social skills: These are the tools that allow us to interact with others effectively, building healthy relationships and resolving conflicts constructively. It is like a set of tools that allows us to build bridges, cultivate friendships and strengthen bonds.

Developing emotional intelligence is like learning a new language, the language of emotions. It is learning to decipher the signals that our body and mind send us, to interpret the nuances of facial expressions and to understand the nuances of human communication.

Emotional intelligence is not an innate gift, but rather a skill that can be learned and developed throughout life. It is like a muscle that is strengthened with exercise and constant practice.

By cultivating emotional intelligence, we open up a range of opportunities for a fuller and more satisfying life. We improve our relationships, increase our ability to deal with stress, make more conscious decisions and achieve our goals more easily.

By incorporating emotional intelligence into our daily lives, we begin to experience a significant transformation in interpersonal relationships and in our connection with ourselves. This ability allows us to see beyond immediate reactions, interpreting emotions as valuable messages that guide our choices and behaviors. It is through this deep understanding that we become more able to create genuine bonds and strengthen mutual trust.

The practice of emotional intelligence also teaches us to find balance amidst life's inevitable challenges. Recognizing and accepting our emotions, without being dominated by them, transforms adverse situations into learning experiences. Thus, each difficulty faced becomes an opportunity to refine our skills and bring us closer to a more complete and resilient version of who we are.

More than an individual skill, emotional intelligence is an invitation to build a more compassionate and collaborative world. By developing our capacity to understand and respect the emotions of others, we contribute to a more harmonious and welcoming environment. It is in this daily practice of empathy, self-awareness and connection that we find the key to a more meaningful and fulfilling life.

Chapter 4
Physiology of Emotions

Emotions transcend the mere domain of the mind, being intrinsically linked to the physical functioning of the body. Every sensation of joy, sadness, anger, or fear triggers measurable physiological responses, impacting heart rhythms, breathing patterns, muscle tension, and even chemical processes in the brain. This phenomenon is not just an automatic reflex, but an intimate interaction between body and mind, where each bodily system contributes to the lived emotional experience. By understanding this connection, we pave the way for more effective management of emotions and their impact on our health and behavior.

The human body operates as an intricate signaling system, manifesting emotions through specific physiological responses. When confronted with a threat, for example, the heart races and breathing becomes rapid, as the body prepares an instinctive defense or flight reaction. Anger, on the other hand, generates intense muscle tension and a noticeable increase in bodily energy, ready to be released. Even more subtle emotional states, such as melancholy or calmness, leave their mark on physiological patterns, revealing a unique bodily choreography that reflects emotions in real time.

Central to this process is the autonomic nervous system, which regulates essential involuntary functions and plays a primary role in emotional response. This system, composed of the sympathetic and parasympathetic branches, is like a conductor orchestrating the dynamics between excitement and relaxation. While the sympathetic drives the body in stressful situations, promoting readiness and vigor, the parasympathetic takes control in moments of tranquility, restoring balance and facilitating physical and emotional recovery. Together, these systems create a complex scenario where each emotion has a distinct physiological "signature," reflecting the harmonious or challenging interaction between body and mind.

Understanding the physiology of emotions allows us to access powerful tools to consciously regulate emotional states. Techniques such as breath control, muscle relaxation exercises, and meditative practices not only calm the nervous system, but also create an internal space for self-reflection and emotional resilience. By becoming more attentive to the language of the body, we discover clearer paths to face emotional challenges, promoting health, balance, and well-being.

Imagine the body as an internal communication system, using physiological signals to express and regulate emotions. The heart races in the face of a threat, breathing becomes shallow in moments of anxiety, muscles tense in response to anger. These signals, often subtle, are like whispers from the body, revealing the secret language of emotions.

The autonomic nervous system, responsible for regulating the body's involuntary functions, plays a central role in orchestrating physiological responses to emotions. It is divided into two main branches: the sympathetic nervous system and the parasympathetic nervous system.

The sympathetic nervous system is 1 like an accelerator, preparing the body for action in stressful or dangerous situations. It increases heart rate, blood pressure, and breathing rate, releasing adrenaline and other hormones that prepare us to fight or flee.

The parasympathetic nervous system, in turn, acts as a brake, promoting relaxation and recovery of the body. It decreases heart rate, blood pressure, and breathing rate, stimulating digestion and rest.

Emotions, therefore, are not just mental events, but also complex physiological processes that involve the interaction between the brain, the nervous system, and the body's organs. Each emotion has a unique physiological signature, a set of bodily responses that characterize it.

Anger, for example, increases heart rate, blood pressure, and muscle tension, preparing the body for action. Fear, on the other hand, can cause palpitations, sweating, tremors, and difficulty breathing, activating the "fight or flight" system.

Sadness, in turn, tends to decrease the body's heart rate and energy, leading to fatigue and apathy. Joy, in contrast, increases the release of endorphins, hormones that promote feelings of pleasure and well-being.

Understanding the physiology of emotions allows us to interpret our body's signals and intervene more effectively in emotional regulation. We can use breathing, relaxation, and meditation techniques to calm the nervous system, reduce stress, and promote emotional balance.

By deepening our understanding of the physiology of emotions, we recognize the body as an indispensable ally in the pursuit of emotional balance. This internal dialogue, translated into physical signals, offers us valuable clues to interpret and manage our responses to everyday situations. Awareness of these processes enables us to intervene more assertively, promoting a harmonious relationship between mind and body.

Practicing mindful listening to the body is an exercise in connecting with our deepest emotional needs. Each accelerated heartbeat, each shortened breath or muscle tension is an opportunity to pause and understand what our body is trying to communicate. This perception opens doors to the adoption of strategies that favor self-regulation, contributing to an emotionally more stable and healthy life.

In the end, understanding the physiology of emotions is embracing the complexity of the human being in its entirety. It is recognizing that emotions do not exist only in our mind, but are lived in every cell of our body. This understanding inspires us to cultivate practices that promote integral well-being, uniting science and consciousness in a journey of self-discovery and balance.

Chapter 5
Thoughts and Emotions

The functioning of the human mind reveals an intricate balance between thoughts and emotions, a relationship that profoundly shapes our experiences and behaviors. Thoughts, like invisible architects, build the foundations of perception and determine the meaning we attribute to events around us. In turn, emotions act as driving forces, imbuing these thoughts with intensity and meaning, transforming them into palpable responses to the environment and circumstances we face. This continuous interaction between what we think and what we feel is not only inevitable, but also fundamental to understanding and influencing the course of our inner life.

Understanding how thoughts originate and impact emotions is essential to dealing with the challenges of the mind. Each thought that occurs in our mind carries with it the possibility of generating corresponding feelings, capable of shaping our state of mind and our attitude towards life. By recognizing that these thoughts are interpretations—and not absolute truths—it becomes possible to take a more active role in directing our mental energy, intentionally choosing those thoughts that favor our growth and emotional well-being.

Thus, awareness of this intricate mechanism allows for the cultivation of a more resilient and balanced mind. Developing skills to observe our thoughts without clinging to them or automatically reacting to the emotions they awaken is a transformative step. With this practice, we are able to reprogram mental patterns, interrupt harmful cycles, and promote an emotional life more aligned with our goals and values. This offers us the opportunity not only to better understand the functioning of the mind, but also to use it as a powerful tool to create a more satisfying and harmonious reality.

Understanding the interaction between thoughts and emotions is essential to unraveling the secrets of the human mind and mastering the art of emotional management. It is like having a map that guides us through the complex landscapes of our inner world, allowing us to navigate with more clarity and awareness through the different nuances of human experience.

Thoughts are like seeds that we plant in our mental garden. Each thought, whether positive or negative, has the power to bear fruit in our emotions and behaviors. Positive thoughts, like flower seeds, cultivate pleasant emotions, such as joy, gratitude, and hope. Negative thoughts, like weeds, generate unpleasant emotions, such as sadness, anger, and fear.

It is important to recognize that thoughts are not facts, but rather interpretations of reality. Our mind, like a filter, processes information from the outside world and shapes it according to our beliefs, values, and past experiences. Two people can observe the same event and have completely different interpretations, generating distinct emotions and behaviors.

Emotions, in turn, influence the way we think. When we are happy, we tend to have more positive and optimistic thoughts. When we are sad or anxious, our thoughts become more negative and pessimistic. It is as if emotions are lenses that color our perception of the world, influencing how we interpret events.

This interaction between thoughts and emotions creates a dynamic cycle. Thoughts generate emotions, which in turn influence new thoughts, and so on. This cycle can be virtuous, when we cultivate positive thoughts that generate pleasant emotions, or vicious, when we let ourselves be carried away by negative thoughts that feed unpleasant emotions.

The good news is that we can learn to interrupt this cycle and reprogram our minds to cultivate more positive and constructive thoughts. Through self-observation, we can identify the patterns of negative thoughts that sabotage us and replace them with more realistic and empowering thoughts.

The constant practice of observing and redirecting one's own thoughts allows us to establish a new mental pattern, where clarity and positivity become natural allies. This process requires patience and dedication, but the fruits harvested—a more serene and balanced mind—justify the effort. Thus, each conscious choice to nurture constructive thoughts becomes a step towards a healthier and fuller emotional life.

By developing this skill, we become active agents in the creation of our internal realities, breaking with automatic cycles that perpetuate suffering and stagnation. This mastery over thoughts and emotions not only promotes individual well-being, but also reflects in our interactions and the impact we have on the world around us.

Finally, understanding and harmonizing the dance between thoughts and emotions is more than a practice; it is an invitation to live with purpose, authenticity, and lightness. This journey, although challenging, reveals to us the transformative power that resides within each of us, ready to be cultivated and manifested in all aspects of life.

Chapter 6
The Language of Emotions

Emotions are universal and profound expressions that reveal the inner state of human beings, transcending cultural and linguistic barriers. They constitute a sophisticated communication system that uses physical, behavioral, and expressive signals to convey crucial messages about our emotional condition and our interactions with the world around us. Deciphering this language is not only a valuable skill but a fundamental need for those seeking emotional balance and self-understanding.

Each emotion is like a unique piece in an emotional puzzle, carrying a distinct set of signals and functions. Anger, fear, sadness, joy, and love are examples of emotional states that have specific patterns of expression and impact. For example, anger often reflects a perception of injustice or violation of boundaries, while fear signals possible threats and the need for self-preservation. Understanding these nuances is like learning the vocabulary of an essential language for emotional self-regulation.

By immersing ourselves in the study of emotions, we develop a kind of "internal dictionary" capable of translating and interpreting what our body and mind are trying to communicate. This ability not only strengthens the relationship with ourselves, but also significantly improves our communication with others, allowing us to respond in a balanced and conscious way to the emotional demands of everyday life.

Just as a linguist dedicates himself to studying the nuances of a foreign language, we must dedicate ourselves to understanding the subtleties of emotional language. Each emotion has its own vocabulary, expressing itself through a unique set of signs and symptoms.

Anger, for example, manifests as a tightness in the chest, an increase in body temperature, a tense facial expression, and an altered voice. Fear translates into palpitations, sweating, tremors, and a need to escape. Sadness is expressed through a tightness in the heart, tears, a downcast facial expression, and a feeling of emptiness.

Joy, in turn, manifests itself with a radiant smile, bright eyes, a feeling of lightness, and vibrant energy. Love translates into warmth in the chest, an affectionate gaze, a desire for closeness, and a feeling of deep connection.

Each emotion, like a word in a dictionary, has its own meaning, a specific function, and a set of messages that it transmits to us. Anger, for example, signals the violation of boundaries or the frustration of needs. Fear alerts us to danger and drives us to seek safety. Sadness invites us to process loss and connect with our vulnerability.

Joy indicates that we are on the right path, that we are experiencing pleasurable and meaningful experiences. Love connects us with what is most important in our lives, drives us to care for and protect those we love.

Understanding the language of emotions is like having an internal translator, which allows us to decipher the messages that our body and mind send us. It is learning to identify the nuances of each emotion, to recognize its signs and to interpret its meanings.

This ability allows us to respond to emotions in a more conscious and constructive way. We can identify the triggers that trigger unpleasant emotions, understand the needs behind them, and develop effective strategies to deal with them.

Delving into the language of emotions is an exercise in self-knowledge that opens doors to a richer and more balanced emotional life. When we become fluent in this internal language, we are able to transform automatic reactions into conscious responses, strengthening both our resilience and the quality of our relationships.

This learning teaches us to welcome each emotion as an ally, rather than an adversary, and to listen to its messages with attention and respect. Thus, anger can become an invitation to establish healthy boundaries, fear can alert us to act with caution, and joy inspires us to pursue what brings us meaning and fulfillment.

Mastering emotional language is more than a path to balance; it is an art that connects us deeply to what it means to be human. It is in this understanding that we find the power to navigate life's challenges with more clarity, cultivating an existence aligned with our values and full of authenticity.

Chapter 7
External Influences

Emotions are shaped by an intricate network of external factors that interact directly with our senses and perceptions. The environment in which we live, the interpersonal relationships we cultivate, and the cultural values we embrace play crucial roles in shaping our emotional state. This continuous interaction reveals how our emotional responses are deeply connected to the world around us, enabling a clearer understanding of the forces that impact our well-being.

The physical environment, with its visible and subtle characteristics, is one of the first influencers to impact our emotions. Organized, well-lit places with harmonious colors have the potential to induce a sense of tranquility and emotional balance. On the other hand, cluttered or noisy places can intensify stress and impair our ability to concentrate. The way we perceive these nuances of the environment directly reflects on our levels of comfort and emotional stability.

In addition, the quality of human connections we maintain is fundamental to balancing our emotions. Healthy relationships, which promote mutual support and genuine exchanges, strengthen our resilience and raise our self-esteem. In contrast, bonds laden with tension and negativity affect our ability to deal with challenges and can amplify feelings of insecurity or sadness. Recognizing and prioritizing interactions that generate well-being is essential to maintaining a healthy and proactive emotional perspective.

Cultural and social patterns form a powerful backdrop to the way we interpret and express emotions. Cultural values establish norms that guide our interaction with the world, creating contexts in which certain emotions are more accepted or repressed. This cultural dynamic shapes not only how we react internally, but also how we connect with others, allowing for a deeper understanding of the emotional diversity that permeates the human experience.

The physical environment in which we find ourselves has a significant impact on our emotions. A peaceful and harmonious environment, with soft colors, relaxing sounds and pleasant aromas, tends to promote feelings of calm and well-being. On the other hand, a chaotic, noisy and polluted environment can generate stress, anxiety and irritability.

Colors, for example, have a language of their own, capable of evoking different emotions. Shades of blue and green convey serenity and tranquility, while shades of red and orange evoke energy and enthusiasm. Lighting also plays an important role: natural light promotes well-being and vitality, while artificial light can cause fatigue and irritability.

Sounds also influence our emotional state. Soft, harmonious music calms the mind and reduces stress, while excessive noise can cause irritation and anxiety.

Aromas also have a power over our emotions: the smell of lavender promotes relaxation, while the smell of lemon stimulates concentration and focus.

Interpersonal relationships are another crucial factor in shaping our emotions. The people we live with, whether family, friends, co-workers or romantic partners, exert a powerful influence on our emotional state. Healthy relationships, based on respect, affection and reciprocity, promote happiness, trust and well-being.

On the other hand, toxic relationships, marked by conflict, manipulation and disrespect, can generate anxiety, sadness, anger and insecurity. It is essential to cultivate positive and nurturing relationships that support us in our challenges and celebrate our achievements.

The culture in which we are inserted also shapes our emotions. Each culture has norms, values and beliefs that influence the way we express and interpret emotions. Some cultures value the open expression of emotions, while others encourage restraint and emotional control.

Culture also influences the way we perceive and interpret the emotions of others. In some cultures, direct eye contact is interpreted as a sign of trust and respect, while in others it can be seen as a sign of aggression or challenge.

Recognizing external influences on our emotions empowers us to take a more active role in the pursuit of emotional balance. By consciously adjusting our physical environment, selecting colors, sounds and elements that promote well-being, we create spaces that support our tranquility and positive energy. This attention to the context around us is an act of self-care and self-knowledge.

In interpersonal relationships, intentionally choosing the bonds we nurture is essential for our emotional health. Surrounding ourselves with people who offer genuine support and reciprocity strengthens our resilience in the face of challenges. Similarly, learning to set healthy boundaries in tense situations protects us from harmful influences and preserves our inner balance.

By understanding the depth of cultural influences, we gain a broader perspective on human emotional diversity. This understanding invites us to be more compassionate, both with ourselves and with others, recognizing that each emotional expression is shaped by a vast landscape of unique contexts and experiences. Thus, the connection between our emotions and the external world becomes a path to living more consciously and harmoniously.

Chapter 8
Positive Emotions

Positive emotions play an essential role in building a balanced and fulfilling life, directly influencing our physical, mental, and emotional well-being. They not only bring moments of joy and contentment but also strengthen our ability to face challenges with optimism and determination. By experiencing emotions such as love, gratitude, hope, and joy, we are developing inner resources that promote resilience and enable us to create deeper connections with the world around us. These emotions are more than mere feelings; they are powerful tools that shape our perception of reality and our ability to flourish in the face of adversity.

The importance of cultivating positive emotions lies in the direct impact they have on our emotional health and quality of life. When we prioritize practices that promote feelings of happiness and gratitude, we are strengthening our brain circuits associated with optimism and satisfaction. Furthermore, positive emotions broaden our worldview, helping us to see opportunities where we once only saw difficulties. This expansion is not just theoretical; it is reflected in concrete actions, such as the willingness to learn new skills, build solid relationships, and contribute to the community. It is through this virtuous cycle that positive emotions create a lasting effect on our journey of personal growth.

To integrate positive emotions into our daily lives, it is essential to recognize them as essential elements of our existence, and not as mere fleeting moments. Simple practices, such as daily reflection on moments of gratitude, the pursuit of authentic connections, and engagement in activities that bring us genuine joy, become essential. Love, for example, can be nurtured by dedicating quality time to the people we cherish, while hope can be strengthened by setting realistic goals and celebrating each achievement, no matter how small. Thus, the continuous cultivation of these emotions prepares us not only to enjoy the good times but also to face challenges with renewed strength and a positive perspective.

Joy is like a contagious melody that invites us to dance through life with lightness and enthusiasm. It emanates from pleasurable experiences, such as a meeting with dear friends, the realization of a dream, or the contemplation of the beauty of nature. Joy energizes us, broadens our perspective, and opens us to new possibilities.

Love is the most powerful force in the universe, an invisible link that connects hearts and drives us to care for, protect, and nurture those we love. Love manifests itself in different forms: romantic love, family love, love for friends, love for animals, and even love for humanity. It inspires us to be better, to forgive, to give, and to build a more compassionate world.

Gratitude is like a balm that heals the soul, soothing the wounds of the past and opening space for the appreciation of the present. It is the ability to recognize and value the blessings of life, from the small joys of everyday life to the great achievements. Gratitude connects us with the abundance of the universe and fills us with hope.

Hope is the flame that guides us in moments of darkness, the compass that guides us towards a better future. It is the belief that, even in the face of challenges and adversities, there is a light at the end of the tunnel. Hope strengthens us, drives us to move forward, and inspires us to build a more promising future.

Cultivating positive emotions is like nourishing our soul with essential nutrients for its growth and development. It is like creating a protective shield against life's adversities, strengthening our resilience and propelling us towards happiness and well-being.

Positive emotions are like seeds that, when cared for with attention, flourish in our inner garden, bringing beauty and balance to our daily lives. Every act of cultivating love, gratitude, hope, or joy is an investment in a richer and more meaningful life, capable of withstanding the winds of hardship. This practice invites us to live with intentionality and genuine connection to what truly matters.

By incorporating these emotions into our routine, we create a solid foundation for building more harmonious relationships, more inspiring projects, and a broader and more welcoming view of life. This change is not just internal; it radiates to those around us, generating a cycle of positivity that transforms not only our experiences but also the environment we share with others.

Finally, by recognizing the transformative power of positive emotions, we embrace the opportunity to become architects of our own well-being. It is in this simple and profound movement that we discover the ability to live fully, navigating life with courage, lightness, and a heart open to the infinite possibilities that it offers.

Chapter 9
Negative Emotions

Negative emotions are fundamental components of the human experience and play a crucial role in our emotional and mental development. Instead of treating them as disturbing forces to be avoided at all costs, it is essential to recognize them as legitimate indicators of our deepest needs, limits, and values. They are not mere adversities that cross our path, but rather messages that, when understood and managed, can guide us towards self-knowledge and personal transformation.

Anger, sadness, fear, and frustration are natural manifestations that help us interpret and react to the world around us. Anger, for example, arises as a direct response to situations of injustice or disrespect, offering an intense energy that, when channeled properly, can be transformed into a driving force for meaningful change. Similarly, sadness should not be seen merely as an emotional burden, but as an opportunity for introspection, an invitation to process painful experiences and find meaning in the midst of adversity.

Fear, often misunderstood, is a powerful survival tool that alerts us to possible dangers and prepares us to act more consciously and carefully. When balanced, it does not paralyze us, but teaches us to face challenges with discernment. Frustration, in turn, calls us to rethink strategies and cultivate resilience in the face of obstacles, functioning as a catalyst for overcoming and learning.

Negative emotions play an indispensable role in our growth journey. Facing them with acceptance and curiosity allows us not only to better deal with challenges but also to develop a richer and more adaptable emotional repertoire. Through this approach, we learn to transform difficulties into opportunities, building a solid foundation for balance and personal fulfillment.

Anger is like a fire that burns within us, an intense energy that drives us to act in the face of injustice, violations of boundaries, or frustrations. It can manifest as a volcanic explosion, with shouting and aggression, or as a silent simmering, with resentment and bitterness. Anger, when expressed in a healthy way, can be a motivating force for change and the pursuit of justice.

Sadness is like a rain that washes the soul, a deep dive into our most vulnerable emotions. It arises in the face of loss, disappointment, and frustration, bringing with it a sense of emptiness and melancholy. Sadness invites us to get in touch with our pain, to process our emotions, and to find meaning in difficult experiences.

Fear is an internal alarm that alerts us to dangers and threats, prompting us to seek safety and protection. It can manifest as a paralyzing anxiety, which prevents us from acting, or as a mobilizing adrenaline, which prepares us to face challenges. Fear, when balanced, helps us survive and make more conscious decisions.

Frustration is like an obstacle that blocks our path, a feeling of helplessness in the face of unachieved goals. It arises when our plans are frustrated, our expectations are not met, or our desires are blocked. Frustration, when well managed, can drive us to seek new strategies, develop our persistence, and strengthen our resilience.

It is important to recognize that negative emotions, like positive ones, have a purpose in our lives. They provide us with valuable information about our needs, our limits, and our values. Instead of trying to suppress or ignore them, we should embrace them, understand them, and use them as tools for self-knowledge and personal growth.

Accepting and understanding negative emotions allows us to transform them into allies rather than adversaries. When we learn to listen to them carefully and react in a balanced way, we discover that they offer us valuable clues about aspects of our lives that need attention or adjustment. This process of acceptance is an essential step for emotional growth and building a healthier relationship with ourselves.

By integrating these emotions into our personal narrative, we recognize their contribution to the formation of our character and resilience. Anger can teach us about boundaries, sadness connects us to the depth of our experiences, fear guides us towards caution, and frustration encourages us to innovate and persist. In each of them, there is a unique opportunity for learning and transformation.

The balance between accepting negative emotions and cultivating positive ones is what leads us to a more authentic and fulfilling life. This journey of self-knowledge prepares us to navigate the emotional tides with courage and wisdom, transforming difficulties into strength and uncertainties into clarity. Thus, each emotion, however challenging, becomes an essential part of the story of who we are and who we can become.

Chapter 10
Emotional Resilience

Emotional resilience is an essential skill for navigating the ups and downs of life, sustained by an inner ability to overcome challenges, cope with adversity, and find learning in every difficult experience. It is a characteristic that allows us not only to withstand storms but also to grow through them, transforming moments of pain and uncertainty into opportunities for evolution. This process involves a combination of self-knowledge, flexibility, and a sense of purpose, which function as the foundations of an inner fortress, designed to face the inevitable impacts of everyday life with balance and determination.

In essence, emotional resilience is the art of standing firm in the face of adversity, without denying the vulnerability that is part of the human experience. It is about recognizing the emotions that arise in difficult times, but using them as fuel to build new perspectives and creative solutions. This inner strength is not innate, but a skill developed with practice, self-compassion, and an ongoing commitment to cultivating positive thoughts, strengthening social connections, and investing in strategies that promote well-being.

With resilience, each difficulty becomes an opportunity to refine our emotional capabilities and prepare us for future challenges. It is a process that invites us to grow from our experiences, continually reconstructing our understanding of ourselves and the world around us.

Emotional resilience is the ability to adapt and overcome adversity, transforming difficult experiences into opportunities for growth and learning. It is like a spring that compresses under pressure but returns to its original shape with more strength and flexibility.

Resilient people are not immune to suffering, but they have an extraordinary ability to deal with difficulties, find meaning in crises, and move forward with courage and hope. They see challenges as opportunities to strengthen, learn, and evolve.

Developing emotional resilience is like building an inner fortress, capable of resisting the attacks of fate. It is like equipping ourselves with armor that protects us from the arrows of suffering, allowing us to maintain balance and serenity even in the midst of storms.

Some pillars of emotional resilience:

Self-knowledge: Understanding your own emotions, limits, and strengths is essential to navigate difficulties with more clarity and awareness.

Self-control: Regulating emotions, preventing them from dominating us, allows us to act with more rationality and effectiveness in the face of challenges.

Optimism: Maintaining a positive perspective, believing in the possibility of overcoming and focusing on solutions, drives us to move forward.

Flexibility: Adapting to changes, reassessing plans and seeking alternatives, allows us to overcome obstacles with more creativity.

Social support: Cultivating healthy relationships, seeking support from friends, family, or professionals, strengthens us in difficult times.

Life purpose: Having clear goals and a sense of purpose gives us direction and motivation to overcome adversity.

Emotional resilience is not an innate trait, but rather a skill that can be developed and strengthened throughout life. It is like a muscle that is strengthened with constant exercise, with the practice of self-compassion, forgiveness, gratitude, and the cultivation of positive thoughts.

Emotional resilience is the art of embracing the impermanence of life, transforming difficulties into steps towards maturity and fulfillment. When we accept challenges as opportunities to expand our understanding and strengthen our inner resources, we create a solid foundation to navigate uncertainties with courage and balance. This process does not eliminate suffering, but reframes it, transforming it into learning and renewal.

By developing this skill, we approach a more authentic version of ourselves, learning to balance vulnerability and strength. Each challenging experience leaves marks that, when integrated with wisdom, enrich our ability to face the ups and downs of the journey. Thus, resilience is not just a defense against adversity, but a bridge to personal growth and connection with what really matters.

Emotional resilience invites us to walk through life with a more open heart and a more flexible mind, always ready to learn, grow, and reinvent. In this constant movement, we find not only ways to survive, but to flourish, even in the most adverse conditions, building a legacy of strength and hope for ourselves and those around us.

Chapter 11
Self-Observation

The practice of self-observation is a process that requires the same attention and rigor that a scientist applies when observing an experiment in a laboratory. Here, however, the laboratory is the mind itself, and the object of study is the thoughts, emotions, and sensations that arise incessantly in our internal experience. This exercise is the essential starting point for those who wish to take control of their emotional life, becoming more aware and able to deal with daily challenges.

By illuminating the inner aspects of our existence through self-observation, we begin to see clearly the patterns that previously went unnoticed. These internal dynamics include recurring thoughts, triggers that trigger emotional reactions, and automatic responses that often put us in cycles of self-sabotage. More than just awareness, this practice transforms us into attentive explorers of our minds, able to map the intricate connections between external stimuli and internal responses.

Developing the ability to observe without judgment is like strengthening a mental muscle. At first, it may seem difficult to stay focused, as our attention is often dispersed among the countless thoughts and emotions that arise. However, with dedication and practice, this skill becomes a powerful tool for understanding and transforming our relationship with the inner world. Each emotion and thought gains a space to be recognized and analyzed, without the pressure of being controlled or repressed.

Self-observation thus creates a pause between what happens to us and how we choose to react. This pause, however small it may seem, is where our freedom and possibility for change reside. It is in this interval that we have the chance to replace impulsive responses with conscious actions, interrupting harmful cycles and cultivating a more balanced and functional emotional state.

Self-observation is like turning on a light in the inner landscape, revealing the contours of our emotional world. It is like becoming an explorer of one's own mind, mapping the unknown territories of our emotions, thoughts, and behaviors. Through self-observation, we can identify repeating patterns, triggers that trigger certain emotions, and automatic reactions that sabotage us.

Developing self-observation is like training an attention muscle, learning to direct focus inward, to the constant flow of our inner experience. It is like becoming a silent observer of one's own thoughts, emotions, and sensations, without judgments or criticism.

At first, the mind may seem like a restless monkey, jumping from branch to branch, from thought to thought, from emotion to emotion. But with constant practice, the mind begins to calm down, and observation becomes clearer and more precise.

We can observe our emotions as a scientist observes a natural phenomenon, without getting involved or trying to control it. We can perceive the physical sensations that accompany each emotion: the tightness in the chest of anxiety, the heat in the face of anger, the tear that runs down in sadness.

We can observe our thoughts as clouds passing through the sky of our mind, without identifying with them or getting carried away by them. We can perceive the negative thoughts that limit us, the repetitive thoughts that bind us to the past, and the anxious thoughts that project us into the future.

Self-observation allows us to create a space between stimulus and reaction, between thought and emotion, between emotion and behavior. This space of awareness gives us the opportunity to choose how to respond to challenges, rather than reacting automatically.

The practice of self-observation invites us to a deep dive into our essence, illuminating what was previously hidden in the shadows of our consciousness. It is in this process of bringing to light the internal patterns that we find the power of transformation, breaking automatic cycles and creating space for choices more aligned with our values and aspirations.

Over time, this skill becomes an inner compass, guiding us to respond to challenges with balance and clarity. What was once a whirlwind of disordered emotions and thoughts transforms into an understandable flow, where each element is recognized as part of a larger and more coherent whole. This attentive look brings us closer to a more conscious and intentional existence.

Finally, self-observation is not just a practice, but a path to inner freedom. It is in it that we discover the strength to live with presence, to embrace our experiences without judgment, and to act with wisdom in the face of circumstances. Thus, we cultivate a deeper and more harmonious relationship with our own mind, paving the way for a more authentic and fulfilling life.

Chapter 12
Mindfulness

The climber scales the mountain with absolute focus on each step, each movement, and each breath. Their attention rests entirely in the present moment, free from distractions with echoes of the past or worries about the future. This state of concentration and presence reflects the essence of mindfulness, a millennial practice that teaches us to cultivate full attention and connection with the here and now. Mindfulness is not just a concept, but a skill that enables us to live with greater awareness, clearly exploring the continuous flow of thoughts, emotions, and sensations that make up our human experience.

Developing mindfulness is like opening a window to our inner reality, allowing us to be attentive and compassionate observers of what is happening inside us. In the fast pace of modern life, we are often carried away by a whirlwind of thoughts about the past or anxious speculations about the future, taking us away from the present. The practice of mindfulness invites us to pause, redirect our focus, and reconnect with the present moment. This return to the immediate experience of life promotes a more harmonious relationship with ourselves and with the world around us.

With regular practice, mindfulness becomes a powerful tool for training the mind, helping us to abandon automatic patterns of distraction and judgment. When walking, we can bring attention to each movement of the body and the sensation of the feet touching the ground. During a meal, it is possible to fully savor each bite, exploring textures, flavors, and aromas with curiosity and gratitude. Even in everyday interactions, mindfulness invites us to listen with genuine attention, creating deeper and more meaningful connections. This practice empowers us to live with more presence, clarity, and balance, valuing the richness of each moment.

Mindfulness is the ability to be present in body and mind in the present moment, without judgment. It is as if we open a window to our inner experience, observing the constant flow of thoughts, emotions, and sensations without identifying with them. It is as if we become a curious and compassionate observer of our own experience.

In the rush of everyday life, it is common to get lost in thoughts about the past or worries about the future. The mind becomes a whirlwind of thoughts, and we disconnect from the present, from the here and now. Mindfulness invites us to return to the present moment, to the direct experience of life in its fullness.

Practicing mindfulness is like training the mind to focus on the present, like a spotlight that illuminates the here and now. It is as if we cultivate selective attention, choosing where to direct the focus of our consciousness.

We can practice mindfulness at any time of day, in any activity. When walking, we can pay attention to each step, to each movement of the body, to the sensations of the feet touching the ground. When eating, we can savor each bite, noticing the textures, flavors, and aromas of food. When talking to someone, we can listen with full attention, without interruptions or distractions.

Mindfulness helps us to develop self-awareness, to recognize our emotions in the present moment, without judgments or impulsive reactions. It allows us to observe the thoughts that arise in our mind, without being carried away by them. It helps us to cultivate acceptance of the present moment, without resistance or attachment.

Practicing mindfulness is like going down the layers of our experience until we reach the core of what it means to be alive. Each moment becomes an opportunity to rediscover the simplicity and depth of being present, whether in an everyday task or in a moment of contemplation. This state of attention reveals to us the hidden richness in details that previously went unnoticed, transforming life into a more vibrant and authentic experience.

By cultivating mindfulness, we train the mind to respond instead of reacting, creating space for more conscious choices aligned with our values. This process of connecting with the present not only reduces anxiety and stress but also strengthens us emotionally, promoting balance amidst the complexities of everyday life.

Mindfulness is, ultimately, an invitation to live with more presence and intention. Through this practice, we learn to relate to our thoughts and emotions in a more compassionate way, integrating body, mind, and spirit in harmony. Thus, each moment of the present becomes a starting point for the transformation and flourishing of a fuller life.

Chapter 13
Conscious Breathing

Breathing is the basis of our existence, a vital process that connects body and mind in an inseparable way. More than an automatic act, it is a direct link to our internal state, offering the opportunity to profoundly influence emotional balance and physical well-being. Recognizing breathing as a powerful ally is the first step in transforming your daily practice into a self-care tool.

By directing our attention to conscious breathing, we establish a deep connection with the present, allowing each inhalation and exhalation to guide us to a state of calm and clarity. This practice is not just an exercise in attention, but an effective resource for controlling the rhythm of inner life, especially in times of emotional or mental challenge. Understanding this dimension allows us to adopt conscious breathing as a practical and accessible instrument to renew energy, reduce tension, and achieve a more balanced state of being.

In this way, conscious breathing presents itself not only as a simple adjustment in the natural rhythm but as a true therapeutic resource, capable of reconfiguring our internal states and reconnecting us with the now. By bringing breathing to the center of our awareness, it becomes an anchor amidst chaos, a reminder that even in the most challenging situations, we have the ability to return to harmony.

Conscious breathing is like tuning a musical instrument, adjusting the rhythm and intensity to create a harmonious melody. It is paying attention to the flow of air that enters and leaves the lungs, observing the sensations of the body with each inhalation and exhalation. It is as if we turn our gaze inward, tuning our attention to the subtle melody of breathing.

In moments of stress, anxiety, or anger, breathing tends to become rapid and shallow, like a sea agitated by strong winds. This change in breathing rhythm sends signals to the brain, activating the sympathetic nervous system and triggering a series of physiological reactions, such as increased heart rate, muscle tension, and the release of stress hormones.

By practicing conscious breathing, we can interrupt this cycle and calm the inner storm. Breathing deeply, slowly, and rhythmically sends signals to the brain that activate the parasympathetic nervous system, responsible for relaxation and body recovery.

Conscious breathing is like a reset button for our nervous system, helping to regulate emotions, reduce stress, and promote inner balance. It is a simple and effective technique that can be practiced anywhere and anytime.

There are several conscious breathing techniques, each with its specific benefits. Diaphragmatic breathing, for example, consists of breathing deeply, using the diaphragm to expand the abdomen with each inhalation.

This technique helps to calm the nervous system, reduce anxiety, and promote relaxation.

Alternate breathing, in turn, consists of inhaling through one nostril and exhaling through the other, alternating nostrils with each breath. This technique helps to balance the cerebral hemispheres, promoting concentration and mental clarity.

Square breathing, also known as 4x4 breathing, consists of inhaling while counting to four, holding the breath while counting to four, exhaling while counting to four, and holding the breath again while counting to four. This technique helps to calm the mind, reduce anxiety, and promote focus.

The practice of conscious breathing reminds us that the power of transformation is within reach of each inhalation. Each technique, whether diaphragmatic, alternate, or square breathing, offers a key to accessing states of greater balance and presence, adapting to the needs of the moment. These practices not only calm the body but also connect us with an inner serenity that we often forget amidst the fast pace of life.

By anchoring ourselves in breathing, we learn to observe our thoughts and emotions without being dragged away by them. This ability gives us a sense of control and tranquility, even in the face of challenging circumstances. Conscious breathing then becomes a guiding thread that leads us back to the present, promoting clarity and renewal in moments of chaos.

Transforming breathing into an intentional practice is a gateway to a fuller and more conscious life. In each respiratory cycle, we find not only a self-care tool but also a powerful reminder that, even in times of adversity, we can always find balance and strength within ourselves.

Chapter 14
Relaxation

Relaxation represents a fundamental need for human well-being, being more than just a simple break from the daily rush. It is an essential state that allows the restoration of body and mind, relieving the impacts of stress and accumulated tensions. We live in a context where the accelerated pace of activities and the constant demand for attention undermine our energies, making it essential to cultivate moments of calm. In these moments, the body resumes its natural balance, creating fertile ground for renewal and resilience in the face of daily challenges.

Upon reaching relaxation, we experience significant changes in our body. Breathing becomes more fluid and controlled, the heartbeat slows down, and the muscles enter a state of relief that favors physical regeneration. These physiological effects translate into a profound well-being, functioning as a bridge that connects us to a state of inner serenity. This practice not only promotes health, but also prepares us to face life with more clarity and disposition, reducing anxiety and enhancing emotional balance.

Incorporating relaxation into the routine is not a superfluous act, but an effective way to maintain health.

There are several approaches that can be adapted to the needs of each individual. Body techniques, such as progressive muscle relaxation, allow us to identify and release areas of accumulated tension in the body. On the other hand, mental practices, such as meditation and creative visualization, promote inner calm and cultivate a more conscious perception of the present moment. By setting aside time for these practices, we are investing in a mental space of tranquility that helps us face challenges with more balance and clarity.

Relaxation is a state of reduced physical and mental tension, a deep rest that allows the body and mind to recover from the wear and tear of everyday life. It is as if we turn off the "do mode" and enter the "be mode", allowing ourselves to simply exist, without pressures or worries.

When we are relaxed, the heart rate slows down, breathing becomes deeper and slower, muscles relax and the mind calms down. It is as if a wave of tranquility spreads through the body, relieving tension and promoting a feeling of well-being.

There are several relaxation techniques, each with its own specific benefits. Some techniques focus on the body, such as progressive muscle relaxation, which consists of sequentially tensing and relaxing muscle groups, promoting body awareness and relief of physical tension.

Other techniques focus on the mind, such as meditation, which consists of calming the mind and focusing on the present moment, cultivating mindfulness and inner serenity. Creative visualization is also a powerful technique, which consists of using the imagination to create relaxing and peaceful scenarios, transporting the mind to a place of peace and harmony.

Relaxation is more than an occasional practice; it is an invitation to recover the natural balance of body and mind amidst the demands of modern life. Each technique, whether physical or mental, teaches us that rest is not passivity, but a vital activity that nourishes our energy and strengthens our resilience. Incorporating it into the routine is an act of essential care that transforms not only moments of tension, but our entire relationship with everyday life.

When we allow relaxation to be a part of our lives, we open space for renewal, creativity and mental clarity. The simple act of slowing down, breathing deeply and reconnecting with the present moment gives us back a sense of control and serenity. It is in this state of calm that we find the strength to face challenges with more balance and discernment.

By embracing relaxation as an intentional and regular practice, we create an inner refuge where we can renew and strengthen ourselves. This conscious choice empowers us to live more fully and harmoniously, reminding us that self-care is the foundation for a life of health and well-being.

Chapter 15
Meditation

Meditation is like a deep encounter with your own being, a space where the frantic rhythm of the world gives way to the transformative silence of introspection. Just as a lake of crystalline waters reflects the sky and the mountains that surround it, meditative practice offers a mirror to the mind, allowing us to see with clarity and serenity what is happening within us. In this state of stillness, we access a tranquility that transcends external noises and connects us to our purest essence, promoting emotional balance and mental clarity.

By immersing ourselves in meditative practice, we cultivate the ability to observe thoughts and feelings without being carried away by them, as if we were witnesses of passing clouds in the sky of the mind. This practice gives us an intentional pause from the incessant flow of stimuli and worries, creating a safe space to explore the depth of consciousness. Here, the restless mind finds rest and the body responds with a feeling of lightness and renewal, as if an invisible weight were gradually removed.

Meditation also acts as a powerful tool to break automatic patterns of thought and behavior. By turning our focus to something simple and constant, like the breath or a mantra, we anchor ourselves in the present moment, disarming the "autopilot" that so often guides our actions. This continuous practice teaches us to embrace the now, finding beauty and meaning in small things and freeing ourselves from the prison of past or future anxieties.

Through consistent practice, meditation becomes more than an exercise; it transforms into a lifestyle, a way of being in the world with presence and purpose. Techniques may vary, but the common goal is the same: to cultivate a state of inner peace that positively impacts all areas of life. By integrating meditation into everyday life, we open the doors to a path of self-knowledge, healing and expansion of consciousness.

Meditation is a practice that consists of calming the mind, focusing attention on a single point, such as the breath, a mantra or an image. By silencing the internal dialogue and disconnecting from external stimuli, we create a space of inner peace and tranquility, where we can observe thoughts and emotions without judgments or impulsive reactions.

It is as if we turn off the "autopilot" of the mind, which keeps us trapped in repetitive thought patterns and conditioned reactions. When we meditate, we become more aware of the constant flow of thoughts and emotions that pass through our mind, without being carried away by them. It is as if we were watching the clouds passing through the sky, without clinging to any of them.

Meditation is not about completely emptying the mind, but about cultivating mindfulness and impartial observation of the thoughts and emotions that arise. It is as if we were creating a space of consciousness, where we can observe the functioning of the mind without identifying with it.

There are several meditation techniques, each with its own specific benefits and approaches. Vipassanā meditation, for example, consists of observing the breath and bodily sensations with mindfulness, cultivating awareness of the present moment. Samatha-vipassanā meditation combines concentration on the breath with observation of thoughts and emotions, promoting mental calmness and understanding of the nature of the mind.

Transcendental Meditation, in turn, uses mantras to calm the mind and induce a state of deep relaxation. Walking meditation consists of walking in silence, paying attention to each step and each movement of the body, cultivating body awareness and presence in the present moment.

Regardless of the technique chosen, regular meditation practice brings numerous benefits to physical, mental and emotional health. Meditation reduces stress, anxiety and depression, improves concentration and memory, strengthens the immune system and promotes general well-being.

Meditation is a constant invitation to return to the essence of the present moment, where the mind finds rest and life reveals its simplicity. Each technique, whether focused on the breath, a mantra or the body in motion, guides us to a state of presence that transcends the worries of everyday life. In this space of stillness, we are able to rebalance our energy and cultivate a renewed sense of clarity and purpose.

Practicing meditation regularly transforms our relationship with thoughts and emotions, allowing us to become more compassionate observers of ourselves. Over time, this practice is reflected in our daily lives, strengthening our ability to face challenges with calm and resilience. It is not just a moment of introspection, but a way to align body, mind and spirit in harmony.

By incorporating meditation into our routine, we open a path of self-discovery and renewal, where each moment becomes an opportunity to flourish. This journey connects us not only with inner peace, but also with the strength and wisdom necessary to live with more presence, balance and authenticity.

Chapter 16
Nonviolent Communication

Nonviolent Communication (NVC) is a practical and transformative approach that allows people to express their needs and feelings with clarity and respect, while at the same time opening themselves up to genuinely understand the perspectives of others. This model of human interaction goes beyond simple dialogue: it promotes deeper connections, offering an effective path to resolve conflicts and build healthy relationships based on empathy and cooperation. Founded on the principles of active listening and mutual understanding, NVC creates an environment where each individual feels valued and understood, opening space for solutions that meet the needs of everyone involved.

Throughout its practice, NVC demonstrates how to replace reactive and often violent communication patterns, based on judgments and criticism, with compassionate language that encourages constructive dialogue. This transformation requires a conscious change: moving away from the automatism of accusations and adopting a posture that values emotional connection and mutual respect. It is not just about avoiding conflict, but about facing differences with a collaborative mindset, making communication an instrument of harmony and growth.

With four structural components - observation, feelings, needs and requests - NVC invites each person to develop a more sensitive and assertive perception of what they communicate and receive. This practice challenges interlocutors to see the facts without emotional distortions or judgments, to recognize their own emotions with authenticity, to identify the needs underlying situations and to articulate objective and achievable requests. By aligning these elements, NVC becomes an accessible and effective tool to transform interactions and create a fairer and more compassionate world.

NVC was developed by psychologist Marshall Rosenberg as a way to promote peace and mutual understanding in conflict situations. It is an approach that is based on objective observation of facts, expression of feelings, identification of needs and formulation of clear and specific requests.

NVC invites us to abandon the language of blame, criticism and judgment, which generate resistance and estrangement, and to adopt a more compassionate and empathetic language, which promotes connection and understanding. It is as if we were exchanging the weapons of verbal violence for the tools of cooperation and constructive dialogue.

The four components of NVC:

1. Observation: Describe the situation objectively, without judgments or interpretations. It is as

if we were making an impartial report of the facts, like a camera that records the scene without giving opinions.

2. Feelings: Express the feelings that the situation awakens in us, in an authentic and vulnerable way. It is as if we were opening our hearts and sharing our deepest emotions, without fear of being judged.

3. Needs: Identify the needs that are behind our feelings. It is as if we were searching for the root of our emotions, understanding what is really important to us in that situation.

4. Requests: Formulate clear, specific and feasible requests that can meet our needs. It is as if we were making an invitation to cooperation, seeking solutions that benefit everyone involved.

The practice of Nonviolent Communication invites us to a new paradigm of interaction, where each conversation becomes an opportunity to build bridges instead of walls. By integrating its principles into everyday life, we learn to approach differences with curiosity and compassion, replacing impulsive reactions with conscious and respectful responses. This process strengthens not only our interpersonal relationships, but also our own connection with the feelings and values that guide our choices.

More than a technique, NVC is a philosophy of life that challenges us to cultivate empathy in all spheres of our interactions. By prioritizing genuine listening and honest expression, we create an environment where collaboration flourishes naturally and conflicts are seen as opportunities for mutual growth. In this space, communication becomes a powerful tool to transform disagreements into understanding and distances into connection.

Adopting Nonviolent Communication is embracing the possibility of a fairer and more harmonious world, where each voice is valued and each need is heard. It is a call to the courage to dialogue with openness and respect, recognizing that, through empathy, we can create more authentic relationships and build a future guided by cooperation and peace.

Chapter 17
Assertiveness

A tightrope walker advances with precision in his walk on the tightrope, maintaining control between firmness and flexibility, sustained by confidence without giving up humility. Similarly, in human interactions, we are able to position ourselves with clarity and respect, reconciling our needs and opinions with the perspectives and demands of others. This essential communication skill, characterized by honesty and mutual respect, is known as assertiveness. Through it, it is possible to strengthen relationships, defend our rights and achieve personal and professional goals without compromising integrity or disrespecting others.

Being assertive is not just about expressing our opinions clearly, but also about doing so in a balanced way, without falling into the extremes of passivity or aggressiveness. It is about finding a middle ground that allows for the defense of one's own interests while recognizing and respecting the limitations and feelings of others. More than a communication technique, assertiveness is a practice that promotes healthy and constructive interactions, fostering mutual trust and strengthening the self-esteem of all involved.

By developing this skill, we discover a new level of interpersonal interaction. We learn to communicate clearly and effectively, avoiding misunderstandings, frustrations or resentments. We become able to say "no" without guilt, present our opinions without hesitation and receive feedback without feeling attacked. Thus, assertiveness is revealed as a foundation for emotional balance and more harmonious relationships, allowing us to navigate safely through the challenges of human connections.

Being assertive is like being a diplomat in our own lives, able to negotiate complex interpersonal relationships with skill and wisdom. It is expressing our needs, desires and opinions clearly and concisely, without aggression or passivity. It is defending our rights without violating the rights of others, seeking solutions that serve everyone involved.

Assertiveness is a balance point between two extremes: passivity, which leads us to silence our needs and submit to the desires of others, and aggressiveness, which leads us to impose our will without considering the feelings of others. The assertive path allows us to navigate between these two poles, expressing our truths with firmness and respect, without fear of displeasing or being rejected.

Developing assertiveness is like learning a new language, the language of self-confidence and mutual respect. It is learning to say "no" without guilt, to express disagreements without hostility, to make requests without demands and to receive criticism without feeling threatened.

Some principles of assertiveness:

Self-knowledge: Recognizing our own needs, values and limits is fundamental to positioning ourselves with clarity and authenticity.

Self-respect: Valuing our opinions and feelings, recognizing that we have the right to express them without fear of being judged.

Empathy: Considering the perspectives and needs of others, seeking solutions that are mutually beneficial.

Clear and direct communication: Expressing our needs and opinions objectively and concisely, without beating around the bush or ambiguities.

Congruent body language: Maintaining an upright posture, direct eye contact and a firm and calm tone of voice, conveying confidence and security.

Assertiveness is more than a communication skill; it is a reflection of the harmony between self-confidence and respect for others. By practicing it, we cultivate a posture that allows us to express our needs without ignoring the emotions and rights of those around us. This approach, based on balance, promotes more transparent interactions, strengthening bonds and creating a space where dialogue becomes a tool for understanding and mutual growth.

When we incorporate assertiveness into our lives, we free ourselves from the weight of automatic reactions, whether of submission or confrontation. We learn to navigate difficult situations with clarity and purpose, keeping the focus on what really matters: the authenticity of our actions and the positive impact of our words. In this process, we not only improve our interpersonal relationships, but also strengthen our self-esteem and confidence in our ability to deal with challenges.

Being assertive is an invitation to conscious authenticity, where communication reflects who we are, while respecting the essence of others. This practice teaches us that, by positioning ourselves with firmness and kindness, we create an environment of trust and mutual respect, essential to build healthy relationships and face the complexities of life with balance and integrity.

Chapter 18
Managing Stress

Maintaining balance amidst the demands and challenges of modern life is an essential skill that can be developed with consistent and effective practices. Just as a tightrope walker crosses a tightrope with concentration and preparation, it is possible to face external and internal pressures by managing stress consciously and strategically. This management not only preserves physical and mental well-being but also enhances the ability to deal with adverse situations, transforming challenges into opportunities for growth.

Stress is a natural biological response and, in moderate doses, can function as a motivator that drives actions and creative solutions. However, when prolonged or reaching intense levels, it becomes a risk factor, compromising health in a broad way. Its impact can be felt on the immune, cardiovascular and digestive systems, in addition to affecting sleep quality and emotional stability. Therefore, learning to control and redirect the manifestations of stress is essential to maintain a balanced life.

By adopting strategies aimed at identifying triggers, cultivating healthy habits and organizing priorities, it is possible to significantly reduce the negative effects of stress. This involves simple but transformative practices, such as implementing routines that value self-care, using relaxation techniques and strengthening interpersonal connections. In this way, stress management ceases to be an occasional response and becomes a daily competence, essential for a fuller and more satisfying life.

Stress is a natural reaction of the body to challenging or threatening situations. It is like an internal alarm that puts us on alert, preparing us to face dangers or flee from them. In small doses, stress can be beneficial, motivating us to act and overcome obstacles. However, when stress becomes chronic and intense, it can have negative consequences for our health, compromising the immune system, increasing the risk of cardiovascular disease, causing digestive problems, insomnia and a host of other problems.

Managing stress is like taming a wild horse, learning to control its energy and direct it towards constructive purposes. It is like being a gardener who takes care of his inner garden, cultivating healthy habits and eliminating the weeds of stress.

Some effective strategies for managing stress:

Identify stress triggers: Recognizing the situations, people or thoughts that trigger stress is the first step to controlling it. It is like mapping the weak points of our "anti-stress shield", so that we can reinforce them.

Develop healthy habits: A balanced diet, regular physical exercise, adequate sleep and relaxation techniques, such as meditation and mindful breathing, are like nutrients for our well-being, strengthening the body and increasing our resistance to stress.

Organize time and activities: Prioritizing tasks, delegating responsibilities and establishing clear boundaries between professional and personal life are like tools to organize chaos, reducing the feeling of overload and increasing our efficiency.

Cultivate optimism and good humor: Facing challenges with a positive perspective, focusing on solutions and cultivating good humor are like rays of sunshine that illuminate the mind, warding off the dark clouds of stress.

Strengthen interpersonal relationships: Cultivating healthy relationships, based on mutual support, trust and affection, is like building a safety net, which supports us in difficult times and gives us strength to overcome challenges.

Seek professional help when needed: If stress becomes chronic and debilitating, do not hesitate to seek help from a mental health professional. It is like looking for an experienced guide to guide us in unfamiliar terrain, helping us find our way back to balance and well-being.

Managing stress is a continuous practice of self-knowledge and balance, which teaches us to respond to the pressures of life with wisdom and resilience. Each strategy adopted, from identifying triggers to implementing healthy habits, brings us closer to a more harmonious life, where stress ceases to be a silent enemy and becomes a controlled and redirected energy.

By strengthening our "inner shield" with self-care practices and human connections, we learn to face challenges without being consumed by them. This allows us to transform moments of tension into opportunities for growth, reinforcing our ability to deal with adversity and broadening our perspective on what really matters.

Taming stress is, above all, an act of caring for ourselves. It is a conscious choice to live lighter and more present, finding balance in the midst of chaos. On this path, we discover that control is not in avoiding stress, but in facing it with courage and clarity, creating a fuller and more resilient life.

Chapter 19
Dealing with Anger

Anger is an undeniable force that emerges as a clear sign that something within us needs attention. When we feel threatened, wronged or frustrated, it arises as an alert, pointing to situations where our limits have been crossed or our needs ignored. This emotion, although often seen as negative, has a vital role: it awakens us to action, encouraging us to face challenges, defend our rights and correct injustices. However, so that its intensity does not dominate us, it is crucial to learn to channel it wisely, transforming its energy into a resource that promotes solutions instead of conflicts.

Dealing with anger does not mean eliminating or denying it, but understanding its origin and respecting its purpose. It is necessary to recognize that it offers us an opportunity for self-knowledge, revealing vulnerabilities, values and what really matters to us. Anger can also strengthen us, motivating us to overcome obstacles and find creative ways to solve problems. Thus, instead of fearing this emotion, we can see it as a powerful tool that, when handled properly, contributes to our personal growth and improves the quality of our relationships.

Effective anger management involves adopting practical strategies that promote balance and clarity in times of tension. This includes identifying the triggers that awaken the emotion, allowing us to anticipate situations of potential conflict and prepare ourselves to react in a more constructive way. It also requires the ability to express feelings assertively, communicating with respect and empathy, without resorting to aggression or repressive silence. In this way, anger ceases to be a destructive element and becomes a catalyst for positive changes, both within ourselves and in the world around us.

Anger is a natural and healthy emotion that arises when we feel threatened, wronged or frustrated. It signals to us that something is not right, that our limits have been violated or that our needs are not being met. Anger can give us the energy we need to defend our rights, protect those we love and fight for what we believe in.

However, when anger is poorly managed, it can become a destructive force, leading us to act impulsively, aggressively and harmfully. Uncontrolled anger can damage relationships, harm health and prevent us from achieving our goals. It is like an uncontrolled fire, which consumes everything in its path, leaving only ashes and destruction.

Learning to deal with anger is like learning to control fire, using it to heat and illuminate, without letting it burn us. It is like being an alchemist who transforms the raw energy of anger into a positive force, capable of propelling us towards growth and transformation.

Some strategies for dealing with anger:

Identify anger triggers: Recognizing the situations, people or thoughts that trigger anger is the first step to controlling it. It is like knowing the weak points of an enemy, so that we can defend ourselves more effectively.

Express anger constructively: Anger does not need to be repressed or explode into aggression. We can express it assertively, communicating our feelings and needs clearly and respectfully. It is like channeling the energy of a volcano to generate electricity, instead of letting it cause destruction.

Develop conflict resolution skills: Learning to negotiate, communicate non-violently and seek solutions that meet everyone involved are essential tools for dealing with situations that generate anger. It is like building bridges over the abysses that separate us, creating paths for understanding and cooperation.

Practice relaxation techniques: Mindful breathing, meditation and other relaxation techniques can help calm the mind and body, reducing the intensity of anger and promoting emotional balance. It is like using water to put out a fire, cooling the heat of anger and bringing inner peace.

Cultivate patience and tolerance: Developing the ability to deal with frustrations, accept differences and forgive are essential qualities to prevent and control anger. It is like building a dike to contain the waters of anger, preventing them from flooding and destroying everything around them.

Seek professional help when needed: If anger is causing significant problems in your life, do not hesitate to seek help from a mental health professional. It is like asking a firefighter for help to control a fire before it spreads and causes irreparable damage.

Dealing with anger is an exercise in self-knowledge and self-control that allows us to transform this intense energy into something constructive and productive. By recognizing its triggers and learning to channel it, we develop the ability to act with balance, promoting changes that respect both our needs and those of others. Thus, anger ceases to be a destructive force and becomes a valuable resource for expression and personal transformation.

When we face anger as an opportunity for growth, we strengthen our ability to face challenges with clarity and purpose. This process teaches us to cultivate healthier relationships, based on empathy and mutual respect, while at the same time improving our ability to resolve conflicts. Anger, when managed wisely, becomes a fuel for positive action and overcoming obstacles.

Finally, learning to manage anger is a journey of balance and resilience. Along the way, we discover that the strength of this emotion does not have to control us, but can be guided by us, illuminating our steps towards a more harmonious and purposeful life.

Chapter 20
Overcoming Sadness

ence, a legitimate and deeply meaningful emotional response to loss and challenges. Instead of being treated as a burden or an obstacle, sadness should be understood as a natural process of healing and transformation. This emotion, as universal as it is unique in each individual, carries the ability to open doors to deep reflection, allowing a more intimate encounter with our own vulnerabilities and strengths. Accepting sadness is recognizing its function as a catalyst for self-understanding, a guide that leads us on a journey of self-discovery and emotional growth.

Far from being a sign of weakness, sadness can be seen as an invitation to balance, an opportunity to re-evaluate priorities and cultivate resilience. When we allow ourselves to fully feel sadness, instead of suppressing or fighting it, we establish a more authentic connection with ourselves and with the world around us. In this state of acceptance, sadness ceases to be a paralyzing weight and becomes an integrating element, a necessary pause to recalibrate our strengths in the face of adversity.

The process of overcoming sadness involves acceptance and conscious action. It is essential to recognize the intrinsic value of this emotion, allowing it to flow without fear or resistance. More than just overcoming, it is about learning to live and grow with it, transforming it into a valuable resource for inner strength. By integrating sadness as part of our history, we are able not only to go through difficult times, but also to build a richer and more meaningful relationship with our existence.

Often, we try to avoid sadness at all costs, as if it were an enemy to be fought. But sadness is not a weakness, but an opportunity to connect with our humanity, to recognize our frailties and to strengthen ourselves in the face of adversity. Sadness teaches us to value life, to cultivate gratitude for happy moments and to find beauty in imperfections.

Overcoming sadness does not mean forgetting it or pretending it does not exist. It is about embracing the pain, allowing yourself to feel it fully and, little by little, transforming it into learning and growth. It is like navigating a rough sea, letting yourself be carried by the waves of emotion, but keeping the rudder firmly towards calm.

Some strategies for overcoming sadness:

Allow yourself to feel sadness: Do not try to repress or ignore sadness. Allow yourself to feel it fully, without judgments or criticism. Cry if you feel like it, talk about your feelings with someone you trust, or express your pain through art, music, or writing. It is like giving space for the rain to fall, allowing it to wash the soul and renew energies.

Take care of yourself: In times of sadness, it is essential to prioritize self-care. Eat healthy, exercise regularly, get enough sleep, and make time for activities that bring you pleasure and relaxation. It is like offering a warm hug to yourself, nourishing your body and soul with love and attention.

Cultivate gratitude: Even in the midst of sadness, try to focus on the good things in life, the people you love, the positive experiences and the small joys of everyday life. Gratitude is like a beacon that illuminates the darkness, reminding us of the beauty and abundance that exist around us.

Connect with others: Seek support from friends, family, or support groups. Sharing your feelings with people who care about you can bring comfort, relief, and a new perspective. It is like joining other people in a dance of life, sharing the steps and supporting each other in difficult times.

Find meaning in pain: Sadness can be an opportunity for reflection, learning and personal growth. Try to find meaning in the painful experience, extracting valuable lessons and transforming pain into strength and wisdom. It is like turning coal into diamond, polishing the pain through reflection and transforming it into something precious and lasting.

Seek professional help when needed: If sadness is persistent and intense, preventing you from living fully, do not hesitate to seek help from a mental health professional. It is like seeking a doctor to treat a deep wound, receiving the necessary care for healing and recovery.

Overcoming sadness is a process of acceptance and transformation that reconnects us with the essence of our humanity. By allowing it to manifest itself without repression, we recognize the richness of its message, which invites us to reflect on our losses, values and the beauty present even in challenging moments. This encounter with sadness does not weaken, but strengthens, revealing layers of resilience that we often did not know.

When we embrace sadness as part of our journey, we discover that it also carries seeds of renewal and learning. Each tear, each moment of introspection brings us closer to a more conscious and authentic version of ourselves. Thus, sadness becomes a starting point for new perspectives, allowing growth to emerge as a natural response to the pain experienced.

Overcoming sadness is not about erasing it, but integrating it into our life path with wisdom and courage. By taking care of ourselves and seeking meaning in our experiences, we transform sadness into a guide that illuminates paths of overcoming, self-understanding and deeper connection with what really matters.

Chapter 21
Overcoming Fear

Fear is a primitive and universal force, present in all human beings, playing an essential role in our survival. It arises as an instinctive response that alerts us to potential threats and prepares us to act, either by fighting or fleeing. However, in its most intense or disproportionate form, fear can exceed its protective purpose and become a significant obstacle. Instead of driving us, it can limit us, blocking our ability to explore, grow and live fully. To overcome fear, it is necessary to understand its nature, take an active stance towards it and use it as a catalyst for personal development and for the achievement of goals that, at first glance, seem unattainable.

First, it is essential to recognize fear as a natural part of the human experience, allowing yourself to embrace this emotion without judgments or resistance. When we accept fear, we open the way to understand it better, identifying its origins and distinguishing what is real from what is imagined. By doing so, we begin to reduce its power of paralysis and place ourselves in a more conscious and empowered position. Overcoming fear is not an act of denial, but of transformation. It ceases to be an uncontrollable monster to become an adversary that we can face and eventually overcome.

Furthermore, it is essential to adopt practical and gradual strategies to deal with the specific fears that prevent us from moving forward. Each step taken in the direction of facing these fears is a victory in itself, strengthening our self-confidence and building a solid foundation for future challenges. The practice of self-care, the cultivation of realistic thoughts and the search for social support are powerful tools that can help us to safely navigate the uncertain territory of fear. In this process, we learn not only to deal with our vulnerabilities, but also to discover strengths that, until then, were hidden.

When we perceive fear as an opportunity for learning and growth, we transform what was once a blockage into a lever for achievement. Facing fear is, ultimately, an act of courage and self-love, an essential step towards inner freedom and the achievement of our true potential.

However, when fear becomes excessive and disproportionate to the real threat, it can become an obstacle that prevents us from living fully, from pursuing our dreams and from reaching our potential. Uncontrolled fear can imprison us in a cage of anxiety, insecurity and limitation. It is as if the dragon of fear kept us chained in its cave, preventing us from flying towards freedom.

Overcoming fear does not mean eliminating it completely, but rather taming it, transforming it from a paralyzing enemy into an ally that drives us to overcome challenges and achieve our goals. It is like riding the dragon of fear, using its strength and energy to reach new heights.

Some strategies to overcome fear:

Face fear gradually: Start by facing your fears in small doses, gradually increasing the level of exposure to the feared situation. It is like climbing a mountain step by step, conquering each stage with safety and confidence, until you reach the top.

Question the thoughts that feed fear: Often, fear is fueled by negative and irrational thoughts, which distort reality and amplify the feeling of danger. Question these thoughts, looking for evidence that confirms or denies them, and replace them with more realistic and positive thoughts. It is like unmasking the illusions created by the dragon of fear, revealing the truth behind the shadows.

Develop self-confidence: Believe in your ability to deal with challenges and overcome obstacles. Remember your past achievements, your skills and your inner resources. Self-confidence is like a sharp sword, capable of cutting the chains of fear and freeing us from its clutches.

Visualize success: Imagine yourself facing the feared situation with courage and success, feeling the sense of freedom and accomplishment in overcoming the challenge. Visualization is like a map that guides us towards our destination, showing us the way forward and inspiring us to achieve our goals.

Practice relaxation techniques: Conscious breathing, meditation and other relaxation techniques can help calm the mind and body, reducing anxiety and fear. It is like creating a protective shield against the dragon's fire, keeping us safe and protected in the midst of the flames.

Seek social support: Share your fears with people you trust, seeking support, understanding and encouragement. Social support is like an army of allies, fighting alongside us against the dragon of fear, giving us strength and courage to win the battle.

Overcoming fear is a journey that begins with acceptance and is strengthened by conscious action. Recognizing fear as a legitimate part of the human experience frees us from the burden of judgment, allowing us to face it with courage and determination. Each small step taken towards facing our fears transforms what was once a barrier into a springboard for personal growth.

This journey requires patience and the practice of strategies that promote self-confidence and emotional balance. By questioning negative thoughts, visualizing success and seeking social support, we cultivate a solid foundation to challenge fear. Each victory, however small it may seem, brings us closer to a fuller life, where fear does not paralyze us, but drives us to explore our potential and go beyond self-imposed limits.

Facing fear is, above all, an act of self-compassion and courage. In this process, we discover that we are stronger than we imagine, and that fear, when faced, can be transformed into a driving force to conquer inner freedom and realize dreams that once seemed unattainable.

Chapter 22
Self-Compassion

Self-compassion is the practice of offering yourself the same care and support you would naturally show a dear friend in a difficult moment. When faced with mistakes, failures, or challenges, it is essential to cultivate an attitude of kindness and understanding towards ourselves, instead of indulging in harsh self-criticism. This approach helps us face suffering in a healthier way, recognizing our shared humanity and allowing us to grow from lived experiences.

Embracing self-compassion means acknowledging that pain and failure are inevitable parts of the human journey, and that this does not make us less valuable. Instead of drowning in feelings of inadequacy, we can support ourselves emotionally, treating our moments of vulnerability as opportunities for learning and strengthening. Just as we would offer a welcoming hug to someone we love, we can be our own source of comfort, accepting our imperfections with empathy and understanding.

When we practice self-compassion, we are strengthening our emotional resilience and expanding our capacity to face adversity. This practice is not just an act of self-care, but a commitment to developing a healthier and more balanced relationship with ourselves. Ultimately, self-compassion helps us live more authentically, recognizing that we are worthy of love and acceptance exactly as we are.

Self-compassion is like a warm hug that we offer ourselves in times of difficulty, a balm that soothes emotional wounds and strengthens us to move forward. It is treating yourself with the same kindness, understanding, and acceptance that you would offer a dear friend.

In a society that often values self-criticism and the pursuit of perfection, we can develop a merciless inner critic that judges, blames, and diminishes us in the face of any mistake or failure. This negative inner voice can lead to self-sabotage, anxiety, and depression.

Self-compassion is the antidote to this destructive self-criticism. It is like silencing the voice of judgment and replacing it with a voice of support, understanding, and acceptance. It is recognizing that we are all imperfect, that we make mistakes and face difficulties, and that this does not make us less worthy of love and compassion.

The three components of self-compassion:

1. Self-kindness: Treating yourself with kindness and understanding, rather than self-criticism and judgment. It's like being a good friend to yourself, offering support and encouragement in difficult times.

2. Shared humanity: Recognizing that suffering is part of the human experience, that we all go through difficult times and that we are not alone in our pain. It is like connecting with the great web of life,

recognizing that we are all interconnected and share the same joys and sorrows.

3. Mindfulness: Observing your own thoughts and emotions with clarity and acceptance, without identifying with them or getting carried away by them. It's like being a curious and impartial observer of your own experience, without judgments or impulsive reactions.

The practice of self-compassion is an act of courage that allows us to transform the relationship with ourselves. When we treat ourselves with kindness and accept our shared humanity, we break the cycle of self-criticism and make room for self-care and growth. This inner acceptance not only relieves suffering, but also gives us strength to face challenges with resilience and serenity.

By cultivating self-compassion, we learn that our imperfections do not define us, but rather how we choose to deal with them. This practice teaches us to seek learning instead of perfection, and to find a balance between striving for improvement and accepting who we are. In this process, we become not only kinder to ourselves, but also more capable of extending that kindness to others.

Living with self-compassion is embracing our journey with authenticity and respect, recognizing that we are worthy of love in all our phases. It is through this practice that we strengthen ourselves emotionally, live with more lightness, and create an inner space where healing, joy, and self-development can flourish.

Chapter 23
Forgiveness

Forgiveness is like the key that frees a soul imprisoned by the weight of resentment and pain. It invites us to let go of the emotional ties that prevent us from living fully, allowing inner peace and freedom to take the place of suffering. Just as a bird recovers its wings when it leaves a cage, the practice of forgiveness transforms our relationship with the past, not erasing mistakes or justifying offenses, but freeing us from the burden they represent.

It is a gesture of deep courage, an act of self-love that involves acknowledging the pain, facing it, and consciously choosing not to let it define our lives. By forgiving, we pave the way for healing and growth, creating space for new possibilities and a more genuine connection with ourselves and others. Forgiving does not eliminate the memory of what happened, but reframes the impact of that past, allowing us to walk lightly towards the future.

When we forgive, we break the invisible chains that bind us to hurts and grudges, replacing those feelings with understanding and compassion. It is a gradual process that requires patience and dedication, but rewards with a sense of relief and reconnection with our purpose and inner peace. Forgiveness, in its essence, is a powerful choice of freedom, which transforms both the giver and the receiver.

Forgiveness is an act of courage and compassion, which frees us from the shackles of the past and allows us to move forward with lightness and serenity. It is a conscious choice to abandon resentment, anger, and the desire for revenge, opening space for healing, reconciliation, and personal growth.

To forgive does not mean to forget or justify the offense, but to free oneself from the weight of the pain and suffering it causes. It is like letting go of the stones we carry on our backs, allowing us to walk with more lightness and freedom.

Forgiveness is a gift we give ourselves, an opportunity to free ourselves from the captivity of the past and build a more positive and promising future. It is like opening the windows of the soul, letting in the light of compassion, healing, and peace.

Forgiving yourself:

Often, we are our own biggest critics, blaming and judging ourselves for past mistakes. Self-compassion and self-forgiveness are essential to free ourselves from guilt and shame, paving the way for learning and growth. It is like offering ourselves the same understanding and kindness that we would offer a dear friend.

Forgiving others:

Forgiving those who have hurt us can be a challenge, but it is an essential step towards healing and emotional freedom. By forgiving others, we free ourselves from resentment and anger, opening space for compassion and reconciliation. It is like breaking the chains that bind us to the past, allowing us to move forward with lightness and serenity.

Forgiveness is a journey of liberation that begins within ourselves. By choosing to forgive, we are not erasing what happened, but reframing the impact that events have had on our lives. This practice teaches us to let go of the weight of the past, allowing the present to be lived with more clarity and lightness. Forgiveness, both for others and for ourselves, is a profound act of self-love and an essential tool for emotional healing.

When we forgive, we open space for more constructive feelings, such as compassion and gratitude. This change allows us to reconnect with our essence, strengthening resilience and expanding our capacity to love and accept, both the imperfections of the world and our own. It is in this movement that we find not only relief, but also the strength necessary to transform pain into learning.

By practicing forgiveness, we take a powerful step towards inner peace. This act teaches us that the past does not have to dictate our future and that, by letting go of the chains of hurt, we gain the freedom to live more fully and truly. Thus, forgiveness becomes a gift we offer ourselves, a portal to healing, and an invitation to renewal.

Chapter 24
Gratitude

Gratitude is a powerful feeling that connects us to the essence of the good things we experience in our lives. Think of each positive experience, each gesture of kindness, as a precious fragment that makes up the mosaic of our existence. Recognizing these pieces, valuing their impact on our journey, is what gives life to the practice of gratitude. More than a simple emotional response, it is a state of consciousness that allows us to see beyond the everyday, revealing the beauty and richness hidden in every detail of our reality.

Gratitude functions as a catalyst for positive emotions, amplifying our sense of connection and belonging. When we reflect on the moments that brought us joy or learning, we strengthen our ability to find meaning even in challenging situations. This genuine recognition not only enhances the luminous aspects of our journey, but also nourishes the ability to transform adversity into opportunities for growth. It is a process that invites us to revisit the present with a renewed perspective, cultivating serenity and resilience.

The continuous practice of gratitude teaches us that every detail - from a simple gesture of kindness to the encounters that shape our history - plays a fundamental role in our well-being. Through it, we discover that true abundance lies not only in great deeds or achievements, but in seemingly ordinary moments that, when valued, are revealed to be extraordinary. Thus, by incorporating gratitude as an integral part of our perspective, we not only acknowledge the blessings that surround us, but also become more receptive to new experiences and possibilities.

Gratitude is a positive emotion that arises when we recognize and appreciate the good things we have in our lives, be they big or small. It is an attitude of gratitude for the gifts we receive, for the people who love us, for the experiences that enrich us, and for the opportunities that come our way.

Cultivating gratitude is like nurturing the soil of this inner garden, allowing the flowers of joy, peace, and well-being to bloom more intensely. It is like opening the heart to receive the blessings of life, recognizing the abundance that surrounds us and cultivating an attitude of appreciation and contentment.

The benefits of gratitude:

Increased happiness and well-being: Grateful people tend to be happier, more optimistic, and more satisfied with life. Gratitude helps us focus on the good things, appreciate what we have, and cultivate a positive outlook.

Improved relationships: Gratitude strengthens bonds, increases empathy, and promotes generosity. When we are grateful for the people in our lives, we feel more connected to them and more motivated to cultivate healthy and positive relationships.

Reduced stress and anxiety: Gratitude helps us cope with adversity, overcome challenges, and find inner peace. When we are grateful, we focus on the blessings in life, which helps us maintain calm and serenity even in difficult times.

Improved physical and mental health: Studies show that gratitude is associated with a number of health benefits, such as lowering blood pressure, strengthening the immune system, improving sleep, and reducing symptoms of depression and anxiety.

How to cultivate gratitude:

Keep a gratitude journal: Take a few minutes each day to write about the things you are grateful for. It can be something simple, like a sunny day, a kind gesture from a friend, or a delicious meal.

Express gratitude to people: Thank the people in your life, expressing your appreciation for their presence, support, and love. A simple "thank you" can make a big difference in someone's life.

Practice mindfulness: Pay attention to the little things in everyday life, the details that often go unnoticed, such as the singing of birds, the smell of rain, or the taste of fresh fruit. Mindfulness helps us recognize the beauty and abundance that surrounds us.

Cultivate an attitude of appreciation: Value the things you have, rather than focusing on what you lack. Remember that many people in the world do not have access to the same opportunities and privileges as you.

Gratitude is a transformative practice that teaches us to appreciate beauty in simple things and find meaning in every aspect of our lives. By acknowledging what we already have and the experiences that have shaped us, we cultivate a state of contentment that transcends external circumstances. This continuous practice strengthens our hearts, opening space for joy and resilience in the face of challenges.

Incorporating gratitude into our routine is an invitation to live with more presence and connection. Whether by keeping a gratitude journal, expressing appreciation to the people around us, or carefully observing everyday details, we discover that abundance is less about material things and more about how we perceive and value our journey. Gratitude reminds us that each moment has its unique and irretrievable value.

Finally, cultivating gratitude is a choice that amplifies our well-being and connects us to the essence of what truly matters. By living with a grateful heart, we not only celebrate the blessings we have already received, but also become more open to receiving new gifts from life, creating a continuous cycle of joy and growth.

Chapter 25
Positive Thinking

Positive thinking is the foundation of a mindset that transforms the way we experience everyday life, illuminating our minds with hope, optimism, and self-confidence. It acts as an inner force capable of nurturing our perspective in the face of difficulties, allowing us to see possibilities where before there seemed to be only obstacles. Just like a gardener who cares for the soil so that the best seeds may flourish, cultivating positive thoughts requires attention, dedication, and conscious choices. This practice does not deny the existence of challenges; on the contrary, it recognizes them as opportunities for growth and learning, promoting an internal transformation that is reflected in all areas of life.

More than a fleeting state of mind, positive thinking is an active stance, a daily decision to focus on available resources, possible solutions, and the favorable aspects of each situation. By adopting this approach, we create a mental space where gratitude, trust, and joy can prosper, allowing us to face adversity with greater clarity and balance. It is as if we were adjusting the lenses with which we see the world, filtering out the excess negativity and letting in the lights of hope and motivation that fuel our ability to act and transform.

With this, positive thinking ceases to be just a personal practice and becomes a powerful force for building a more satisfying and meaningful life. It enhances our resilience, improves our physical and mental health, and contributes to strengthening the bonds in our relationships. Moreover, it inspires us to move forward with courage and creativity, exploring innovative paths and embracing new possibilities. Thus, the decision to cultivate a positive mindset is not just an exercise in immediate well-being, but a long-term investment in the development of a full, harmonious existence connected to our deepest aspirations.

Positive thinking is a mental perspective that focuses on the favorable aspects of life, on possibilities, solutions, and available resources. It is a way of seeing the world through rose-colored glasses, filtering out negativity and hopelessness, and making room for joy, gratitude, and optimism.

Cultivating positive thinking does not mean ignoring problems or pretending that life is perfect. It is about choosing to focus on the opportunities, solutions, and lessons that each situation, however challenging, can offer us. It is like being an alchemist who transforms the lead of difficulties into the gold of wisdom and growth.

The benefits of positive thinking:

Increased resilience: People with a positive mindset tend to be more resilient, overcoming adversity more easily and learning from difficult experiences.

Positive thinking gives us the strength to move forward, even when the path is arduous and full of obstacles.

Improved physical and mental health: Studies show that positive thinking is associated with a number of health benefits, such as stress reduction, strengthening the immune system, improving sleep, and reducing symptoms of depression and anxiety.

Increased creativity and productivity: Positive thinking stimulates creativity, innovation, and the search for solutions. When we believe in our potential and the possibilities that present themselves, we feel more motivated to act, create, and produce.

Improved relationships: Positive thinking makes us more pleasant, optimistic, and receptive to others. When we cultivate a positive mindset, we attract positive people and relationships into our lives.

How to cultivate positive thinking:

Identify and challenge negative thoughts: Pay attention to the thoughts that arise in your mind and identify those that are negative, pessimistic, or self-critical. Question these thoughts, looking for evidence to confirm or deny them, and replace them with more realistic and positive thoughts.

Practice gratitude: Focus on the good things you have in your life, the people you love, the positive experiences, and the small joys of everyday life. Gratitude is a powerful antidote to negativity and hopelessness.

Visualize success: Imagine yourself achieving your goals, overcoming challenges, and living the life you desire. Creative visualization is a powerful tool for programming the mind for success and attracting positive results.

Surround yourself with positive people: Seek the company of optimistic, cheerful, and inspiring people. Positive energy is contagious, and being surrounded by positive people can help you cultivate a more optimistic mindset.

Take care of your physical and mental health: A healthy diet, regular exercise, adequate sleep, and relaxation techniques, such as meditation and mindful breathing, are essential for maintaining emotional balance and cultivating a positive mindset.

Positive thinking is a powerful tool that allows us to transform challenges into opportunities and adversity into learning. Cultivating this perspective helps us find balance and strength even in the most difficult moments, guiding us to creative solutions and a renewed sense of purpose. Thus, optimism is not just a state of mind, but a daily choice that nourishes our well-being and enhances our actions.

By incorporating positive thinking into our routine, we adjust the way we interact with the world, strengthening our bonds and promoting a more constructive approach to situations. This practice inspires us to move forward with confidence and determination, creating a cycle of resilience, growth, and gratitude that connects us with the best of ourselves and others.

The decision to cultivate positive thinking is not just an act of self-care, but a commitment to a more harmonious and satisfying life. By choosing to see the bright side of experiences, we plant the seeds for a meaningful existence, where each challenge becomes an opportunity to flourish and reach new possibilities.

Chapter 26
Emotional Management in Relationships

Interpersonal relationships can be compared to a garden that flourishes with diversity, each flower representing a unique aspect of our human connections. For this garden to thrive, it is essential to dedicate care, attention, and nurture interactions with positive and reflective attitudes. Emotional management emerges as the main tool to promote this care, allowing us to manage conflicts, foster empathy, and create a fertile environment for strengthening bonds.

By applying the principles of emotional management, we acquire the ability to transform challenges into opportunities for mutual growth. Each interaction can be seen as an invitation to exercise understanding, express needs respectfully, and practice patience. Thus, the bonds of trust and affection are cultivated firmly, even in terrain that initially seems arid or difficult to manage.

In this way, learning to manage emotions is not just a skill, but a continuous investment that directly reflects the quality of our romantic, family, friendship, or professional relationships. With dedication, we build a harmonious space where genuine exchange and mutual understanding become the most precious fruits of our emotional cultivation.

In relationships, whether they be romantic, family, friendship, or professional, emotions play a fundamental role. They influence how we communicate, how we deal with conflicts, and how we build bonds of affection and trust. Emotional management allows us to navigate the complex dynamics of relationships with more awareness, balance, and wisdom.

Some principles of emotional management in relationships:

Self-knowledge: Understanding your own emotions, needs, and limits is the first step to building healthy relationships. It's like knowing the soil of our own garden, so that we can cultivate the right plants and offer them the proper nutrients.

Empathy: Putting yourself in the other person's shoes, understanding their emotions, needs, and perspectives, is essential to create genuine connections and strengthen emotional bonds. It is like tuning in to the melody of the other's heart, creating a harmony that enriches the relationship.

Assertive communication: Expressing your own needs and opinions clearly, respectfully, and authentically is fundamental to avoid misunderstandings and build relationships based on trust and reciprocity. It's like using a common language, which allows both sides to understand and connect with each other.

Conflict management: Conflicts are inevitable in any relationship, but how we deal with them can strengthen or weaken bonds. Emotional management allows us to face conflicts with calm, respect, and a search for solutions that meet both sides. It's like pruning the weeds in the garden without damaging the delicate flowers.

Forgiveness and reconciliation: Making mistakes is part of human nature, and in relationships, forgiveness and reconciliation are essential to overcome hurts and restore harmony. It is like fertilizing the garden soil after a storm, allowing the flowers to bloom again with more vigor.

Emotional management in relationships is a continuous process of care and improvement, which allows transforming each interaction into an opportunity for a deeper and more meaningful connection. By cultivating self-knowledge, empathy, and assertive communication, we create fertile ground for bonds to grow with respect and authenticity, even amidst the natural challenges of living together.

By dealing with conflicts in a balanced way and seeking reconciliation through forgiveness, we open space for relationships to not only survive, but thrive. These practices strengthen trust and create an environment where emotions can be expressed and understood in a healthy way, reinforcing the importance of dialogue and collaboration.

Emotional management in relationships is, above all, an act of love - for ourselves and for others. It is the commitment to nurture each bond with attention and respect, allowing the garden of our connections to flourish with harmony and beauty, even in the face of adversity that arises along the way.

Chapter 27
Emotional Management in the Family

The family is the essential foundation for human development, a space where we learn the basics of emotions, coexistence, and affection. In this nucleus, daily interactions shape our ability to deal with feelings, resolve conflicts, and build healthy relationships. Just as a plant needs constant care to grow and flourish, family life requires deliberate attention for its relationships to be strengthened. By understanding and practicing emotional management on a daily basis, it is possible to transform family dynamics into an environment of mutual growth, respect, and genuine love.

Emotional management in the family context requires each member to take an active role in promoting more conscious and compassionate interactions. This implies cultivating habits that value open communication and the recognition of emotions, both one's own and others'. Instead of suppressing conflicts or difficult emotions, it is necessary to face them as learning opportunities, strengthening bonds and creating an atmosphere of emotional security. This approach ensures that everyone, from children to adults, feels respected and supported in their personal development journey.

By taking care of family relationships with empathy and responsibility, we are also investing in a positive emotional legacy for future generations. Children who grow up in emotionally healthy environments learn to build more balanced relationships and face challenges with resilience. Parents and caregivers, in turn, have the opportunity to directly influence the creation of a solid foundation of love and respect, which will be reflected in their own lives and in society as a whole. Therefore, emotional management in the family is not just an individual practice, but a collective commitment that transforms and enriches the lives of everyone involved.

Emotional management in the family is like the art of gardening applied to family relationships. It is learning to identify the needs of each member, to nourish the soil of communication, to prune the branches of conflicts and to reap the fruits of love, respect and harmony.

Cultivating emotional intelligence in the family:

Affectionate communication: Expressing love, affection, and appreciation for each other is fundamental to create a climate of affection and security in the family. It's like watering the garden with words of encouragement, gestures of affection, and tight hugs.

Active listening: Listening carefully, without judgment or interruption, is essential to understanding the emotions and needs of each family member. It is like leaning in to hear the murmur of the wind among the leaves, capturing the subtle messages it brings.

Empathy: Putting yourself in the other person's shoes, trying to understand their feelings and perspectives, is fundamental to building bridges of connection and resolving conflicts peacefully. It is like putting yourself in the shoes of the flower that opens to the sun, feeling its fragility and its strength.

Conflict management: Disagreements and conflicts are inevitable in any family, but how we deal with them can strengthen or weaken family ties. It is important to learn to express emotions assertively, to negotiate and to seek solutions that meet everyone's needs. It's like pruning branches that grow erratically, without hurting the trunk of the tree.

Setting boundaries: Setting clear and consistent boundaries is essential for the healthy development of all family members. It's like building a fence around the garden, protecting it from external threats and allowing plants to grow safely.

Family traditions and rituals: Creating family traditions and rituals, such as having dinner together, celebrating special dates, or sharing leisure time, strengthens emotional bonds and creates positive memories. It's like decorating the garden with elements that bring beauty, meaning, and personality.

Quality time: Setting aside time to live together, play, and have fun together is essential to nurture family relationships. It's like sitting in the shade of a leafy tree in the garden, enjoying the beauty of the present moment and the company of those we love.

Emotional management in the family is a continuous practice of care and connection that transforms the home into an environment of mutual growth and unconditional love. By cultivating affectionate communication, active listening, and empathy, we create a space where each member can feel welcomed and valued, allowing for a more harmonious and enriching coexistence.

When we face family challenges with patience and commitment, we learn to transform conflicts into opportunities for learning and strengthening bonds. Each gesture of understanding, each limit established with respect, and each tradition cultivated reinforce the emotional foundation that sustains the family, creating a legacy of love and resilience for future generations.

Investing in emotional management in the family context is an act of collective transformation that is reflected in every aspect of life. By nurturing these relationships with care and attention, we not only strengthen the family nucleus, but also contribute to forming more empathetic, resilient individuals who are prepared to build a more balanced and compassionate world.

Chapter 28
Emotional Management at Work

The work environment is a space where emotions play a central role, directly influencing interactions and outcomes. Each professional is part of a dynamic ecosystem, where how emotions are managed can determine individual and collective success. Emotional management emerges, in this context, as an essential skill, capable of transforming daily challenges into opportunities for growth and overcoming. Recognizing the impact of emotions in the corporate environment is the first step in cultivating resilience, strengthening interpersonal relationships, and boosting productivity.

Daily, professionals face pressures such as challenging deadlines, unexpected changes, and the need to balance ambitious goals with personal demands. In these situations, emotional management acts as a guide, helping to identify and regulate one's own emotions and respond to those of others with empathy and assertiveness. This competence not only promotes inner balance but also strengthens the sense of team, facilitating clear communication, effective collaboration, and constructive conflict resolution.

By integrating emotional intelligence into the corporate environment, it is possible to create a healthier and more engaged organizational culture. This involves cultivating self-awareness to understand automatic reactions, adopting practices that minimize stress, and developing a leadership style that inspires confidence and motivation. Thus, the workplace ceases to be a merely functional space and transforms into an environment where human potential is fully explored, promoting professional achievements aligned with emotional well-being.

In the work environment, we are constantly exposed to situations that challenge our emotional balance: tight deadlines, challenging goals, fierce competition, interpersonal conflicts, unexpected changes. Emotional management allows us to navigate these challenges with more serenity, resilience, and intelligence.

Mastering the professional stage with emotional intelligence:

Self-awareness: Understanding your own emotions, triggers, and behavior patterns is essential to identify strengths and weaknesses and develop strategies to deal with work pressures. It's like knowing your own character, your motivations, your fears, and your desires, to interpret it with authenticity and mastery.

Stress management: Developing mechanisms to deal with stress, such as relaxation techniques, time organization, and cultivating healthy habits, is fundamental to maintaining emotional balance and high productivity. It's like preparing the body and mind for performance, ensuring that the actor has the energy and focus to shine on stage.

Assertive communication: Communicating clearly, directly, and respectfully, expressing ideas, opinions, and needs constructively, is essential for building healthy and productive professional relationships. It's like mastering the art of dialogue, using your voice and body language to convey messages with clarity and impact.

Teamwork: Collaborating with colleagues, sharing responsibilities, respecting differences, and seeking solutions together is essential to the success of any team. It's like creating a symphony on stage, where each instrument contributes to the harmony of the whole.

Compassionate leadership: Leaders who inspire, motivate, and support their teams, creating a positive and collaborative work environment, tend to achieve extraordinary results. It's like being the conductor of the orchestra, leading the musicians with passion and precision, extracting the best from each one.

Conflict management: Conflicts are inevitable in the work environment, but how we deal with them can make the difference between success and failure. Emotional management allows us to face conflicts constructively, seeking solutions that benefit everyone involved. It's like transforming conflict into an opportunity for growth, learning, and improvement.

Emotional management at work is a transformative skill that empowers us to face the challenges of the corporate environment with balance and purpose. By developing self-awareness, we improve our ability to understand and regulate our emotional reactions, making us more resilient in the face of daily pressures. This practice not only strengthens our individual performance but also promotes a healthier and more collaborative organizational climate.

By adopting assertive communication and cultivating teamwork, we create a space where ideas flow freely, relationships thrive, and goals are achieved efficiently. Leaders who integrate emotional management into their leadership style inspire confidence and motivation, transforming their teams into true engines of innovation and sustainable results.

The practice of emotional management at work is, above all, an investment in well-being and human potential. It teaches us that it is possible to balance ambitious goals with quality of life, transforming the workplace into an environment of learning, growth, and achievement, where each challenge becomes an opportunity for collective and personal progress.

Chapter 29
Emotional Management in Education

The classroom is an environment where learning is built based on the interaction between emotions and knowledge. Here, emotions are not just passing influences; they directly shape the ability to concentrate, retain information, and motivate students. Emotional management, in this context, assumes a fundamental role, functioning as a foundation that strengthens interpersonal bonds and enhances curiosity and enthusiasm. Through intentional practices, it creates a space of trust and collaboration, where each student is encouraged to explore their abilities and fully develop their potential.

This process goes beyond the simple application of teaching methodologies; it involves creating an emotionally safe climate where students feel comfortable expressing their ideas and emotions. When emotions are understood and respected, it becomes possible to channel them positively, transforming challenges into opportunities for growth. Thus, the classroom becomes a place where exchanges of experiences and interpersonal relationships create fertile ground for the flourishing of learning. Each interaction, whether between students or between teachers and students, contributes to building an environment based on empathy and mutual respect.

By integrating emotional management as a central part of educational practice, not only is academic performance promoted, but also the development of social and emotional skills essential for life. The ability to recognize, understand and regulate emotions is a skill that benefits students inside and outside of school, preparing them to face challenges with resilience and build healthier relationships. In this way, emotional management transforms the classroom into a dynamic and inclusive space where learning is seen as a continuous process, interconnected with the emotional experiences and personal growth of each individual.

Emotional management in education goes beyond teaching academic content. It is about offering children and adolescents the tools they need to understand and deal with their emotions, develop empathy, build healthy relationships, and become resilient, responsible, and happy adults.

Cultivating emotional intelligence in schools:

Create an emotionally safe environment: A welcoming, respectful, and bullying-free school environment is essential for students to feel safe to express their emotions, share their ideas, and seek help when they need it. It's like building a protected greenhouse where seedlings can grow without fear of bad weather.

Teach emotional recognition and regulation skills: Children need to learn to identify, name, and deal with their emotions healthily. Playful activities, games, and play can be used to teach about emotions in a fun and engaging way. It's like offering an illustrated guide to the world of emotions, with maps and tools to explore each feeling.

Develop empathy: Encouraging children to put themselves in others' shoes, to understand different perspectives, and to show compassion is essential for building healthy relationships and a more just and supportive society. It's like planting seeds of empathy in the heart of every child, which will germinate into fruits of understanding and solidarity.

Promote assertive communication: Teaching children how to communicate clearly, respectfully, and effectively, expressing their needs, opinions, and feelings constructively, is fundamental to preventing and resolving conflicts peacefully. It's like offering an instruction manual for communication, with tips and examples for a more fluid and harmonious conversation.

Encourage self-esteem and self-confidence: Believing in yourself, recognizing your talents, and feeling capable of achieving your goals are fundamental pillars for healthy development and success in life. It's like nourishing the roots of self-esteem so that the plant of the "I" grows strong and confident.

Encourage cooperation and teamwork: Learning to work in a group, share ideas, respect differences, and seek solutions together are essential skills for success in academic and professional life. It's like creating an ecosystem in the garden, where different species coexist in harmony, exchanging nutrients and strengthening each other.

Emotional management in education is the basis for building an environment where learning and human development go hand in hand. When students feel emotionally safe, they not only learn better but also develop essential life skills such as empathy, resilience, and assertive communication. This approach transforms the classroom into a space where challenges become opportunities for growth, and interactions promote meaningful and lasting bonds.

By teaching emotional regulation skills and encouraging empathy, we prepare students to deal with their emotions healthily, promoting a collaborative and respectful environment. These practices not only strengthen academic performance but also create a solid foundation for healthier interpersonal relationships and a more compassionate view of the world.

Integrating emotional management into education is investing in the future of each student, promoting a learning journey that transcends curricular content. It is about empowering future generations to face challenges with confidence and create a positive impact on society, where knowledge is aligned with emotional well-being and solidarity.

Chapter 30
Emotional Management and Mental Health

The human mind is an intricate and fascinating system, where each thought, emotion, and behavior plays a fundamental role in the balance and harmony of the individual. Mental health represents the state of stability of this system, a delicate interaction that promotes well-being, clarity, and functionality in everyday life. Emotional management, in turn, is the conscious practice of understanding and directing emotions to strengthen this stability. Together, these dimensions form the basis for a full existence, allowing each person to reach their maximum potential and navigate life's challenges with resilience and purpose.

Maintaining mental health requires constant attention, like caring for a living organism that responds to internal and external stimuli. Recognizing the signs of imbalance, cultivating healthy habits, and seeking support when needed are essential steps in preserving this state of balance. Emotional management, in this context, acts as an indispensable tool, helping us to deal with stressful situations, strengthen interpersonal bonds, and transform adversity into learning. It is through this practice that we develop self-awareness and improve our ability to manage our reactions to the various experiences we have.

By understanding the importance of mental health and emotional management, it is possible to perceive how these dimensions are intrinsically connected to overall well-being. The ability to identify, regulate and express emotions in a balanced way contributes to building healthier relationships, greater productivity, and a sense of purpose. Just as a harmonious system depends on each component functioning in a coordinated manner, human life benefits from a healthy and emotionally aligned mind. With dedication and conscious practices, we can create a fertile inner environment where positive emotions flourish and human potential is fully realized.

Mental health and emotional management are closely intertwined, like roots intertwining in the soil of our existence. The ability to understand, regulate and use emotions intelligently is essential to maintain mental balance, prevent disorders and build a healthier, happier and more meaningful life.

Taking care of the garden of the mind:

Recognizing the signs: Just as the plants in a garden show signs of imbalance when they are not being well cared for, our mind also sends us messages when something is not right. Insomnia, anxiety, irritability, difficulty concentrating, loss of interest in things that used to give us pleasure - these are some of the signs that may indicate that we need to pay more attention to our mental health.

Cultivating healthy habits: A balanced diet, regular exercise, adequate sleep, contact with nature, and positive interpersonal relationships are like essential nutrients for the garden of the mind, promoting well-being and emotional resilience.

Developing self-awareness: Observing your own thoughts, emotions, and behaviors with attention and without judgment allows us to identify negative patterns and develop strategies to deal with them in a healthier way. It's like studying the garden map, identifying the areas that need more attention and care.

Managing stress: Chronic stress is like a plague that can infest the garden of the mind, causing damage and imbalances. Learning to deal with stress through relaxation techniques, time organization, and seeking social support is essential to maintaining mental health.

Cultivating positive emotions: Emotions such as joy, gratitude, love, and hope are like flowers that beautify and perfume the garden of the mind. Cultivating these emotions through practices such as meditation, contact with nature, and artistic expression promotes well-being and happiness.

Seeking professional help: Just as a gardener may need expert help to combat a persistent pest, we may also need to seek support from mental health professionals when we face emotional difficulties or mental disorders. There is no shame in asking for help, and seeking treatment is an act of courage and self-love.

Emotional management and mental health are fundamental pillars for a balanced and fulfilling life. By developing the ability to recognize and regulate our emotions, we strengthen not only our resilience in the face of challenges but also the ability to fully enjoy moments of joy and fulfillment. This continuous practice teaches us that taking care of the mind is as essential as taking care of the body, creating a solid foundation for integral well-being.

When we cultivate healthy habits, seek self-awareness, and learn to manage stress, we create an internal environment where mental health can flourish. This process is positively reflected in our relationships, productivity, and the way we see the world, promoting a more authentic connection with ourselves and with others. Furthermore, recognizing the need for professional help is a vital step in overcoming difficulties, demonstrating courage and commitment to our own happiness.

Taking care of mental health is an act of self-compassion and responsibility. By integrating emotional management into our routine, we are investing in an internal garden where positive emotions have space to flourish, and challenges can be transformed into opportunities for learning and growth. This conscious choice guides us to a more harmonious, full life aligned with our purpose.

Chapter 31
Self-Esteem:
Building the Foundation of Confidence

Self-esteem is the fundamental structure that supports confidence and each person's ability to face life's challenges. It is a personal assessment that reflects the value we attribute to our existence, encompassing the recognition of our strengths, limitations, and potential. Healthy self-esteem allows us to understand and accept who we are in essence, while cultivating a deep sense of self-love and respect. This process involves continuous effort, patience, and dedication, serving as the solid foundation upon which we build the confidence necessary to live fully and resiliently.

Building self-esteem begins with self-knowledge, which is the central pillar of this process. Understanding our own thoughts, emotions, values, and beliefs allows us to identify and strengthen the positive aspects that make up our identity, as well as courageously face the areas that demand growth. This journey of self-discovery creates fertile ground for cultivating self-love, an essential element for treating ourselves with kindness, valuing ourselves without resorting to perfection. To love oneself is to accept that each person has unique qualities, which are the basis of what makes us unique and worthy of respect.

Furthermore, the practice of acceptance, positive affirmations, and continuous care for physical and emotional well-being reinforce the construction of solid self-esteem. By celebrating achievements, learning from mistakes, and taking care of our needs, we establish a relationship of trust with ourselves. This foundation not only sustains us but also propels us to face challenges and embrace opportunities, shaping a richer, more confident, and fulfilling life.

Self-esteem is the assessment we make of ourselves, the value we attribute to our own existence. It is the basis of confidence, resilience, and the ability to face life's challenges with courage and optimism. Healthy self-esteem allows us to accept our imperfections, recognize our talents, and believe in our potential to achieve our goals.

Building the castle of self-esteem:

Self-knowledge: The first step to building solid self-esteem is to know yourself deeply, exploring your thoughts, emotions, values, beliefs, and motivations. It is like studying the map of your inner castle, identifying your strengths, your weaknesses, and the treasures hidden within.

Self-love: Loving yourself is the mortar that binds the bricks of self-esteem. It is treating yourself with kindness, understanding, and respect, accepting your imperfections and celebrating your qualities. It is like decorating your castle with affection, creating a cozy and welcoming environment.

Acceptance: Accepting yourself as you are, with your flaws and qualities, is essential to building genuine and lasting self-esteem. It is like recognizing the unique beauty of your castle, with its tall towers and hidden basements, without trying to turn it into something it is not.

Positive affirmations: Repeating positive affirmations about yourself, such as "I am capable," "I am brave," "I am worthy of love," is like engraving empowering messages on the walls of your castle, reinforcing your self-confidence and self-love.

Taking care of yourself: Taking care of your physical, mental, and emotional health is like keeping your castle clean, organized, and protected. Eat well, exercise, get enough sleep, cultivate healthy relationships, and spend time on activities that bring you pleasure and relaxation.

Celebrating achievements: Recognizing and celebrating your achievements, no matter how small, is like adding new towers and flags to your castle, symbolizing your growth, your strength, and your ability to overcome.

Learning from mistakes: Making mistakes is part of the learning and growth process. Instead of blaming yourself for mistakes, see them as opportunities to learn, develop, and become a better person. It is like rebuilding a part of your castle with more wisdom and experience, making it even stronger and more resilient.

Self-esteem is the foundation that supports our confidence and drives us to live with authenticity and courage. Building it is a continuous process of self-discovery and acceptance, in which we learn to value our qualities, embrace our imperfections, and cultivate a healthy relationship with ourselves. When we strengthen this foundation, we find the strength necessary to face challenges and transform each experience into learning.

Self-love, caring for our needs, and celebrating achievements are fundamental bricks for erecting the castle of self-esteem. By reinforcing these pillars with self-knowledge and positive affirmations, we create a solid structure that protects us from adversity and allows us to grow with resilience and purpose. Thus, each step taken towards acceptance and respect for who we are becomes an investment in a fuller and more meaningful life.

With healthy self-esteem, we are better prepared to face the world and connect with others genuinely. This foundation allows us not only to believe in our potential but also to inspire confidence and positivity in our relationships, shaping a journey rich in achievements and inner peace.

Chapter 32
Confidence:
Developing Inner Strength

Confidence is an unshakeable inner strength, comparable to a majestic tree that grows firm and resilient, with roots deeply embedded in the soil of self-esteem. It is the solid foundation that enables us to face challenges, achieve dreams, and recognize our intrinsic worth. Just as a tree flourishes when well cared for, confidence expands when cultivated with conscious and continuous practices. Strengthening this inner strength is a transformative process that requires self-knowledge, courage, and perseverance.

More than a mere belief in our abilities, confidence is the concrete expression of the security we feel in ourselves, regardless of circumstances. It manifests itself in the conviction that we are capable of learning, growing, and overcoming adversity. When we develop confidence, we establish an unbreakable foundation for personal fulfillment and for facing the world with determination and purpose. It is this confidence that allows us to act, even in the face of the unknown, with optimism and resilience.

As we embark on this journey of strengthening confidence, it is essential to recognize that each step taken - be it a success or a lesson learned - contributes to this growth. Self-esteem acts as the fertile ground that supports this construction, while the recognition of our talents and achievements serves as nourishment for our development. By overcoming challenges and celebrating victories, we learn to expand the boundaries of confidence, allowing it to fully flourish and become a constant ally in our journey to success and personal fulfillment.

Confidence is the belief in our own abilities, qualities, and judgments. It is the certainty that we can handle the situations that life presents us, overcome obstacles, and achieve our goals. Confidence is a source of empowerment, which drives us to act with courage, determination, and optimism.

Cultivating the tree of confidence:

Nurturing self-esteem: Self-esteem is the fertile ground where confidence takes root. To develop confidence, it is essential to cultivate healthy self-esteem, based on self-knowledge, self-love, and acceptance. It is like preparing the ground for planting, ensuring that the tree has a solid foundation to grow.

Recognizing your talents and abilities: Identifying your strengths, your qualities, and your areas of excellence is like discovering the seeds of confidence that already exist within you. Value your talents, develop your skills, and use them to your advantage.

Celebrating achievements: Each achievement, no matter how small, is like a branch that strengthens in the tree of confidence. Acknowledge your successes, celebrate your victories, and use them as motivation to move forward.

Learning from mistakes: Mistakes are like winds that can shake the tree of confidence, but they don't have to bring it down. See mistakes as learning opportunities, extract valuable lessons, and use them to strengthen and grow.

Stepping out of your comfort zone: Facing new challenges, trying new things, and putting yourself in situations that require courage and overcoming is like expanding the roots of confidence, exploring new territories, and strengthening the base of the tree.

Visualizing success: Imagining yourself achieving your goals, overcoming obstacles, and living the life you want is like nourishing the tree of confidence with the sunlight of hope and optimism.

Cultivating positive relationships: Surrounding yourself with people who believe in you, who support you and encourage you is like creating an ecosystem favorable to the growth of confidence. Seek the company of positive, inspiring people who help you flourish.

Confidence is the force that drives us to explore the unknown, face challenges, and move forward with determination. Just as a tree grows towards the sky when well cared for, confidence flourishes when we nourish our roots with self-esteem, recognize our abilities, and cultivate the courage to act. Each experience of overcoming and each achievement reinforces this foundation, making it more solid and resilient.

To develop confidence, it is essential to celebrate both victories and lessons learned from mistakes. This practice transforms each step, however small, into an opportunity for growth. Stepping out of your comfort zone, surrounding yourself with supportive people, and visualizing our successes are powerful ways to expand this inner strength, allowing it to guide us towards our dreams and aspirations.

Confidence is not a point of arrival, but a continuous journey of strengthening and self-discovery. By cultivating it with intention and consistency, we build a solid foundation that allows us to live with authenticity and purpose, facing life with courage and optimism, while inspiring others to do the same.

Chapter 33
Motivation:
Awakening the Inner Strength

Motivation is the essential force that drives us daily, a powerful and vibrant energy that connects us to our goals and gives meaning to our actions. It manifests as an internal state that guides our choices, reinforces our determination, and provides us with the energy necessary to face challenges and seek personal and professional fulfillment. Awakening this inner strength requires a deep dive into understanding our values, dreams, and purposes, transforming it into a constant and renewing flame that guides each step of our journey.

The ability to stay motivated is directly linked to the clarity of our goals and their alignment with what truly matters to us. When we know exactly what we want to achieve and recognize the importance of these goals in our lives, motivation becomes not just a tool, but an intrinsic part of who we are. It is reinforced by self-confidence, the practice of celebrating achievements, and the continuous pursuit of inspiration and learning. This inner strength does not arise spontaneously but is cultivated through conscious actions that strengthen our resilience and our ability to act proactively, even in the face of adversity.

To build and maintain high motivation, it is essential to establish a favorable environment, both internally and externally. Internally, we must nurture the belief in our abilities, developing self-efficacy and practicing the recognition of our achievements, however small. Externally, it is necessary to seek support from positive and inspiring people, organize the space around us to promote focus and productivity, and adopt habits that reinforce our commitment to progress. Thus, we transform motivation into a fuel that not only sustains our journey but also drives us to go beyond where we imagined we could reach.

Motivation is an internal state that drives us to action, that gives us energy and direction to achieve our goals. It can be intrinsic, when it comes from within, from the pleasure and satisfaction of performing an activity, or extrinsic, when it is driven by external rewards, such as recognition, promotion, or material rewards.

Lighting the flame of motivation:

Defining clear and achievable goals: Having well-defined goals, challenging but realistic, is like charting the route to your destination, giving direction and purpose to your journey. Vague and undefined goals are like sailing without a compass, getting lost in the sea of indecision.

Connecting with your values: When your goals are aligned with your values and beliefs, motivation flows more naturally. It's like sailing with the wind in your favor, driven by a greater force that gives you meaning and purpose.

Finding your purpose: Discovering your "why," the reason why you do what you do, is like discovering the inexhaustible source of motivation. Purpose gives meaning to your journey, turning obligations into missions and tasks into opportunities to contribute to something greater than yourself.

Cultivating self-efficacy: Believing in your ability to achieve your goals is like strengthening the sails of your ship, allowing it to sail with more speed and safety towards your destination. Self-efficacy is the confidence in your own abilities, which drives you to act with determination and persistence.

Celebrating small victories: Recognizing and celebrating each stage overcome, each obstacle overcome, is like refueling your ship, keeping motivation burning throughout the journey. Small victories fuel self-confidence and the drive to move forward.

Seeking inspiration: Reading books, watching movies, talking to inspiring people, and connecting with stories of overcoming is like observing the stars in the sky, guiding yourself by their light and finding new directions for your journey. Inspiration renews energy and fuels the flame of motivation.

Creating a motivating environment: Surrounding yourself with positive people, organizing your workspace, setting challenging goals, and rewarding yourself for your efforts are like creating an environment conducive to navigation, with favorable winds, calm seas, and a motivated crew.

Motivation is the vital force that moves us to achieve, overcome, and transform dreams into reality. Cultivating it is a continuous exercise of alignment between our goals and values, recognizing in personal purpose the most powerful source of inspiration. When we understand the "why" of our actions, every effort gains meaning, and even the most difficult challenges become necessary steps on a journey full of purpose.

Keeping motivation alive requires strategies that reinforce both self-confidence and clarity of path. Celebrating small achievements, seeking inspiration, and creating a supportive environment are practices that renew energy and help us stay committed to our goals. Each victory, however small it may seem, strengthens our determination, while overcoming obstacles reinforces the belief in our abilities.

By awakening and nurturing motivation, we transform our inner strength into a constant flame, capable of illuminating our path even in moments of uncertainty. This energy drives us to go further, exploring our potential and living with passion and purpose, ready to face whatever lies ahead.

Chapter 34
Creativity:
Awakening the Imaginative Potential

Creativity is an essential element of human nature, a dynamic force that permeates all aspects of our lives, shaping the world in which we live. It is not a privilege reserved for a few, but a universal ability, present in everyone, waiting to be explored and expanded. By understanding creativity as a powerful current that flows incessantly within us, it is possible to recognize its fundamental role in problem-solving, innovation, and individual expression. This chapter is an invitation to unlock this potential, removing the obstacles that repress it and allowing it to manifest fully and meaningfully.

Creativity goes beyond mere daydreams; it is deeply connected to the ability to see possibilities where there were once limitations. This ability can be awakened through deliberate practices that stimulate the mind and expand the horizon of ideas. The first step to nurturing creativity is accepting that it is not an innate or exclusive talent, but an aptitude that can be developed. Just as a river gains strength when its paths are clear, our creativity is strengthened by overcoming internal barriers, such as fear of judgment, excessive self-criticism, or attachment to rigid patterns.

The journey to awaken creative potential begins with concrete actions that involve exploring the world around us and seeking inspiration from diverse sources. Whether questioning usual assumptions, experimenting with new approaches, or diving into unknown fields, every effort to break the boundaries of conventional thinking opens new doors for the imagination. This process not only connects us with original ideas but also reinforces confidence in our intuitive abilities and the transformative power of innovation. By cultivating these habits and adopting an open and curious attitude, creativity ceases to be a sporadic flow and becomes a constant force that enriches all aspects of our lives.

Creativity is not a gift exclusive to artists and inventors; it is an inherent ability of all human beings, a dormant potential that can be awakened and developed. It is like a seed that awaits the ideal conditions to germinate and flourish.

Unblocking the flow of creativity:

Cultivate curiosity: Curiosity is the spark that ignites the flame of creativity. It is the desire to explore, to discover, to question, to go beyond the obvious. Be curious like a child, asking "why?" to everything, investigating the world around you with the eyes of a discoverer.

Break with patterns: Creativity flourishes when we free ourselves from the bonds of conventional thinking, judgments, and limiting beliefs. Dare to think outside the box, question the rules, experiment with new approaches, explore alternative paths.

Embrace diversity: Creativity feeds on the diversity of ideas, perspectives, and experiences. Seek inspiration from different sources, talk to people from different cultures and backgrounds, explore different art forms and expressions.

Give wings to the imagination: Imagination is the engine of creativity, the ability to create mental images, to visualize possibilities, to dream of the new and the unusual. Give wings to your imagination, allowing yourself to explore fantastic worlds, create stories and characters, and bring original ideas to life.

Trust intuition: Intuition is the inner voice that guides us towards the best solutions, the most creative ideas, and the most innovative paths. Learn to listen to your intuition, trust your insights and follow your instincts.

Experiment and make mistakes: Creativity is a process of experimentation, trial and error. Don't be afraid to make mistakes, to try new things, to step out of your comfort zone. Every mistake is a learning opportunity, one more step towards mastery.

Cultivate flow: The state of flow is a state of deep concentration, total immersion in the activity, loss of notion of time and space. It is in this state that creativity flows with more intensity and freedom. Look for activities that provide you with this state of flow, such as music, art, writing, sports, or any other activity that you are passionate about.

Creativity is a transformative force that connects us with the unlimited potential of our minds, allowing us to see the world through new and innovative lenses. Cultivating it is an exercise in curiosity, courage, and openness to the unexpected. By exploring ideas, experimenting, and allowing ourselves to make mistakes, we give space for the imagination to flourish, illuminating our paths with original solutions and authentic expressions.

Awakening creativity begins with breaking down internal barriers, such as fear of failure or rigidity of thought. By embracing diversity, trusting intuition, and seeking the state of flow, we broaden our mental horizons and open doors to possibilities that previously seemed unattainable. Each new challenge or experience can be transformed into fuel for creation, as long as we approach it with a curious and receptive mind.

By incorporating creativity as a continuous habit, it ceases to be just a sporadic skill and becomes a living force that transforms the way we live and interact with the world. This imaginative potential not only enriches our lives but also empowers us to leave our unique mark on the universe, innovating and inspiring around us.

Chapter 35
Spirituality and Emotional Management

Spirituality presents itself as an intrinsic aspect of the human experience, a vast horizon that transcends the limits of the tangible, connecting us to values, purposes, and dimensions that enrich our existence. In this context, emotional management emerges as a fundamental skill, which allows us to face life's challenges with resilience while cultivating a state of inner peace. Together, spirituality and emotional management form a solid foundation for a balanced life, allowing us to move forward on our journey with clarity and serenity.

The spiritual quest is not just a connection to something greater, but also a reflection of our desire for self-knowledge and meaning. At the same time, emotional management equips us to deal with the inevitable fluctuations of our emotions, such as anger, fear, and sadness, making us more aware of our inner universe. This interaction between the two aspects invites us to explore a path where ethical values, compassion, and gratitude become compasses that guide our daily choices and strengthen our relationships.

By recognizing the interdependence between spirituality and emotions, we build a foundation that helps us cultivate virtues such as unconditional love, generosity, and humility. The practice of meditation, prayer, or simple contemplation becomes a window to the transcendent, expanding awareness and promoting emotional balance. Personal transformation, in turn, emerges from this process, motivating us to overcome internal challenges and align ourselves with a higher purpose, based on authenticity and connection.

This chapter explores this enriching dynamic, showing how integrating spirituality and emotional management can guide us towards a fuller and more meaningful life.

Spirituality and emotional management complement each other like two sides of the same coin. Spirituality connects us with values and purposes that transcend the ego, inspiring us to cultivate qualities such as compassion, gratitude, forgiveness, and unconditional love. Emotional management provides us with the tools to deal with the challenging emotions that arise along the way, such as fear, anger, sadness, and doubt, allowing us to navigate the turbulences of life with more serenity and balance.

Exploring the inner universe:

Connection with the sacred: Spirituality connects us with a sacred dimension of existence, whether through religion, meditation, contemplation of nature, or other practices that bring us closer to the transcendent. It is as if we open a window to infinity, expanding our consciousness and filling us with peace and serenity.

Search for meaning: Spirituality drives us to seek meaning in life, a purpose that goes beyond material and selfish issues. It is as if we are looking for our own star in the sky, a guide that guides us on our journey and gives us direction.

Cultivation of values: Spirituality inspires us to cultivate values such as love, compassion, gratitude, forgiveness, generosity, and humility. These values are like compasses that guide us in our choices and actions, leading us towards a more ethical, just, and compassionate life.

Self-knowledge: Spirituality invites us to a deep reflection on ourselves, our beliefs, our values, and our role in the world. It is as if we were taking a journey of discovery to our own inner universe, exploring our lights and shadows, our strengths and weaknesses.

Emotion management: Spirituality provides us with tools to deal with challenging emotions, such as fear, anger, sadness, and insecurity. Practices such as meditation, prayer, and cultivating gratitude help us calm the mind, find inner peace, and cultivate emotional resilience.

Personal transformation: Spirituality drives us to a constant search for growth and personal transformation. It is as if we are always in motion, evolving towards a more authentic, compassionate, and conscious version of ourselves.

The integration between spirituality and emotional management leads us to a path of balance, self-knowledge, and a deeper connection with life. By cultivating spirituality, we find a foundation that helps us face challenges with purpose, while emotional management empowers us to deal with the nuances of our emotions, transforming inner turmoil into learning and serenity. This combination prepares us to navigate the complexities of existence with clarity and resilience.

Spiritual practices, such as meditation, prayer, or contemplation, create a space for us to expand our consciousness and cultivate virtues such as compassion and gratitude. At the same time, by managing our emotions with intention, we strengthen our ability to act in alignment with our values and purpose, even in times of uncertainty or difficulty. This cycle of connection and transformation promotes a more authentic and meaningful life.

By aligning spirituality and emotional management, we discover a path to transcend our limitations and connect with something greater. This journey not only elevates us individually but also inspires the creation of more harmonious relationships and a more conscious contribution to the world around us. With this integrated approach, we live more fully, nurturing both our spirit and our emotions.

Chapter 36
Body and Mind:
The Dance of Well-being

The body and mind are inseparable partners, acting in synchrony that reflects the essence of well-being. This deep connection reveals that caring for the body is more than simply strengthening muscles or improving physical conditioning; it is offering the necessary foundation for the mind to flourish in balance and serenity. Likewise, nourishing the mind goes beyond stimulating creative thoughts or achieving emotional tranquility; it is also cultivating an inner strength that sustains the health and vitality of the body. Thus, harmony between body and mind is not just a desirable goal, but an essential choreography that shapes the quality of life as a whole.

A healthy body provides the vigor and energy needed to face daily challenges, while a balanced mind guides us with clarity and determination. When both are in sync, it is as if each aspect of the human being functions as part of a large gear, moving fluidly and efficiently. Therefore, practices that promote this integration – from mindful eating to stress management – should be seen not as obligations, but as acts of self-care and self-love. By strengthening the body and nourishing the mind, we create the ideal conditions for a full existence, in which each movement and thought reflects vitality, serenity, and purpose.

Throughout this chapter, we will explore practical and accessible ways to cultivate this vital interaction between body and mind. We will unveil how small changes in routine can transform the way we live, allowing each choice and action to contribute to a higher state of health and well-being. As in dance, where each step has a purpose and contributes to the beauty of the whole, integrating healthy habits into everyday life is the secret to achieving balance and fulfillment in all areas of life.

Physical and mental health are intimately connected, like two sides of the same coin. A healthy body provides a solid foundation for a balanced mind, while a healthy mind positively influences the functioning of the body. Cultivating habits that promote physical and mental well-being is like perfecting the choreography of life, creating a fluid, elegant, and vital dance.

Tuning body and mind:

Mindful eating: Nourishing the body with healthy and nutritious food is like offering the dancer the fuel needed for their precise and energetic movements. A balanced diet, rich in fruits, vegetables, and whole grains, provides the essential nutrients for the proper functioning of the body and mind.

Regular physical exercise: Regular physical exercise is like the dancer's rehearsal, strengthening their muscles, increasing their flexibility, and giving them resistance and vitality. Physical exercise releases endorphins, hormones that promote a feeling of well-being and reduce stress and anxiety.

Restorative sleep: Sleep is the time for rest and recovery of the body and mind, like a break from dancing to recharge the batteries. Getting enough sleep is essential for memory consolidation, mood regulation, and emotional balance.

Stress management: Chronic stress is like an injury that prevents the dancer from moving with fluidity and grace. Learning to deal with stress through relaxation techniques, meditation, and mindful breathing is essential to keep the body and mind in harmony.

Contact with nature: Connecting with nature is like taking the dance to an inspiring setting, where fresh air, sunlight, and natural beauty invigorate the body and mind. Spending time outdoors, walking in parks and gardens, observing the sky and the sea brings inner peace and renews energy.

Cultivating healthy relationships: Positive interpersonal relationships are like dance partners who support, inspire, and motivate us. Cultivating healthy relationships with family, friends, and colleagues contributes to emotional well-being and happiness.

Creative expression: Creative expression, whether through art, music, writing, or any other form of artistic manifestation, is like giving freedom to the dancer's soul, allowing them to express their emotions, thoughts, and individuality.

The dance of well-being, where body and mind connect in perfect harmony, is not a distant goal, but a continuous process, made of conscious choices and habits that sustain our vitality. Every little action, from a moment of deep breathing to a step towards a more active life, contributes to strengthening this essential link.

By allowing ourselves to listen to what our body and mind need, we adjust the rhythm of this choreography. The integration between simple practices, such as meditation and physical exercise, and the appreciation of moments of pause, teaches us that balance is a dynamic and adaptable movement, not a static goal.

Thus, cultivating this synchronicity is more than an act of self-care; it is a commitment to a fuller and more meaningful existence. As in a well-rehearsed dance, every effort transforms into grace, and every moment becomes part of a life lived to the fullest.

Chapter 37
Food and Emotions: Nourishing the Body and Mind

Eating is more than just ingesting nutrients; it is a sensory and emotional experience that connects body and mind in an essential harmony. Every food choice we make directly influences our energy, mood, and ability to face daily challenges. Thus, understanding the relationship between what we eat and how we feel is essential to cultivate health and emotional balance. The practice of mindful eating allows us to transform meals into moments of care and well-being, helping to align our eating habits with the pursuit of a fulfilling life.

This intimate relationship between food and emotions works in both directions. The nutrients we ingest provide the substrate for fundamental biological processes, such as the production of neurotransmitters responsible for regulating mood, sleep, and the ability to concentrate. On the other hand, emotional states, such as stress or sadness, can lead us to seek comfort in less healthy foods, creating a cycle that can negatively impact both physical and mental health. Recognizing these interactions is the first step towards more conscious and balanced choices.

Adopting a balanced approach means seeing food as an act of integral care. Incorporating nutrient-rich foods that promote mental health, such as those that aid in the production of serotonin or maintain a healthy gut microbiota, is essential. At the same time, practices such as mindfulness during meals and moderate consumption of sugars and fats are tools that help maintain a continuous state of well-being. Thus, each meal becomes an opportunity to nourish not only the body, but also the mind and emotions, promoting a healthier and more harmonious life.

The relationship between food and emotions is a two-way street. Just as the foods we eat can affect our emotional state, our emotions can also influence our food choices. In times of stress, anxiety, or sadness, we may seek comfort in foods high in sugar, fat, or salt, which provide a feeling of immediate pleasure but can have negative health consequences in the long run.

Harmonizing the banquet of life:

Nutrients and neurotransmitters: The foods we eat provide the essential nutrients for the production of neurotransmitters, chemicals that regulate mood, sleep, concentration, and other brain functions. The consumption of foods rich in tryptophan, such as bananas, milk, and eggs, for example, favors the production of serotonin, a neurotransmitter related to well-being and happiness.

Sugar and mood: Excessive sugar consumption can cause spikes in blood glucose, followed by sudden drops, which can lead to irritability, anxiety, and mood swings. It's like an energy roller coaster, with ups and downs that unbalance the body.

Healthy fats and mental health: The consumption of healthy fats, such as those found in fish, olive oil, avocado, and nuts, is essential for the proper functioning of the brain and the prevention of mental disorders, such as depression and anxiety.

Food and gut microbiota: The gut microbiota, composed of trillions of bacteria that inhabit our gut, plays an important role in mental health. A diet rich in fiber, probiotics, and prebiotics favors the balance of the microbiota, which can contribute to the reduction of stress, anxiety, and depression.

Mindful eating: Practicing mindfulness during meals, paying attention to the flavors, aromas, and textures of food, and chewing calmly and consciously, promotes satiety, digestion, and the pleasure of eating. It's like turning the meal into a ritual of gratitude and connection with the present.

Balance and moderation: The key to a healthy and balanced diet is moderation and variety. Avoid restrictive diets and radicalism, and seek a diet that provides you with pleasure, energy, and well-being.

Food, by reflecting our emotions and directly impacting our health, becomes a fundamental link between body and mind. Each food choice is an invitation to balance our emotional states and strengthen the body, transforming the act of eating into a tool for self-care and self-knowledge.

Recognizing the body's signals and the emotions that guide us towards certain food choices is a powerful step towards harmony. When we become aware of these interactions, we expand our ability to make decisions that nourish not only the physical but also the soul, cultivating balance and satisfaction at all levels.

Thus, by combining knowledge about food and mindfulness of our emotional needs, we create a path where health and pleasure go hand in hand. Each meal becomes a moment of celebration and connection, reaffirming the commitment to a full and nourished life in every way.

Chapter 38
Physical Exercise and Emotions: In Motion for Well-being

The body is a complex machine, capable of responding in extraordinary ways to the stimulus of movement, and physical exercise is the key to unlocking its full potential. Each gesture, each coordinated effort, generates a profound impact not only on physical functioning but also on the emotional state, promoting an essential harmony between body and mind. The regular practice of physical exercise goes beyond physical preparation; it is a transformative process that strengthens resilience, enhances vitality, and nourishes emotional well-being, bringing balance and lightness to everyday life.

The connection between physical activity and emotions reveals itself as a continuous and powerful exchange. Just as movement can be a catalyst for feelings of joy, relief, and accomplishment, our emotional states, in turn, shape the way we engage in sports. When we feel strengthened by motivation or confidence, physical exercise becomes a fluid and pleasurable experience. On the other hand, in the face of periods of stress or low energy, it can be a real challenge

- but still an opportunity to transform these negative emotions.

Finding a meaningful approach to integrating physical activity into your routine is critical to exploring its many benefits. From the release of endorphins, which promote well-being and pain relief, to improved sleep quality and strengthened social connections, each aspect reinforces the positive impact of moving the body. More than an act of self-care, exercising is a commitment to integral health and an invitation to transform the relationship between body and emotions into an inexhaustible source of balance and happiness.

The relationship between physical exercise and emotions is a two-way street. Just as physical activity can positively impact our emotional state, our emotions can also influence our willingness to exercise. When we are motivated, happy, and confident, exercising becomes more enjoyable and natural. On the other hand, in times of stress, anxiety, or sadness, we may feel unmotivated and lacking the energy to move.

Finding the rhythm of well-being:

Endorphins and well-being: During physical exercise, the body releases endorphins, a neurotransmitter that promotes feelings of pleasure, well-being, and pain reduction. It is as if the body rewards us for the effort, with a dose of joy and satisfaction.

Stress and anxiety reduction: Physical exercise is a powerful ally in combating stress and anxiety. Physical activity helps regulate the production of stress hormones, such as cortisol, and promotes muscle and mental relaxation.

Improved self-esteem and self-confidence: Regular physical exercise contributes to improved body image, increased self-esteem, and the development of self-confidence. Feeling good about your body and perceiving your ability to overcome challenges brings a sense of empowerment and well-being.

Increased concentration and focus: Physical activity improves blood circulation and oxygenation of the brain, which contributes to increased concentration, focus, and memory.

Improved sleep: Regular physical exercise promotes deeper and more restful sleep, essential for the recovery of body and mind.

Socialization and connection: Practicing exercise in groups, such as in dance classes, yoga, or team sports, promotes socialization, interaction, and the development of healthy relationships.

Finding the ideal activity: Choosing a physical activity should take into account your interests, preferences, and physical condition. Try different modalities and find the one that gives you pleasure, motivation, and well-being.

Movement is a universal language of the body, a way to express and transform emotions. Each exercise performed with intention connects our physical limits to emotional possibilities, creating a virtuous cycle of energy and balance that impacts all spheres of life.

Embracing physical activity as part of everyday life is recognizing its power to rebuild and strengthen both body and mind. Even on the most challenging days, small gestures of movement can act as catalysts for internal changes, dissipating tension and opening space for well-being.

By finding the activity that resonates with your passions and needs, you transform exercise into a ritual of celebrating your own strength. In this process, the body becomes more agile, the mind clearer, and the heart lighter, aligning for a journey of integral health and continuous joy.

Chapter 39
Sleep and Emotions: The Symphony of Rest

Sleep is a vital experience that acts as a foundation for the balance of body and mind, promoting regeneration, serenity, and the organization of emotions. It plays a fundamental role in maintaining our emotional health, functioning as a natural mechanism of adjustment and healing for the impacts of everyday life. With a direct influence on the quality of life, sleep organizes and synchronizes the functions of the body, creating a solid foundation for us to face the challenges of each new journey. The way we sleep reflects, in many aspects, the internal harmony necessary to live with fullness and energy.

The connection between sleep and emotions is intrinsically complex, revealing a two-way relationship that profoundly affects overall well-being. Adequate rest regulates not only cognitive processes but also sustains emotional stability, strengthening resilience against stress, anxiety, and daily adversities. In contrast, sleep deprivation disrupts this balance, resulting in emotional instability, irritability, and difficulty concentrating. Sleep, therefore, emerges as an indispensable ally for a healthy and peaceful mind.

Prioritizing an environment and habits that promote restful sleep is essential to optimize its benefits. A peaceful environment, relaxing routines before bed, and proper management of emotions prepare the ground for more restorative nights. In addition, recognizing when emotional or physical factors consistently interfere with sleep and seeking specialized help are fundamental steps to protect this vital dimension of life. After all, sleep is the basis of our inner harmony, allowing body and mind to operate in sync for a balanced and fulfilling existence.

The relationship between sleep and emotions is a delicate and profound dance. Just as a bad night's sleep can affect our mood, concentration, and ability to deal with emotions, emotional balance also influences the quality of our sleep. When we are anxious, stressed, or sad, sleep can become fragmented, shallow, and unrestful.

Composing the melody of sleep:

Sleep and emotional regulation: During sleep, the brain processes the emotions experienced throughout the day, consolidating memories, regulating mood, and restoring emotional balance. A good night's sleep allows us to wake up more willing, serene, and prepared to deal with the challenges of everyday life.

Sleep deprivation and irritability: Lack of sleep can lead to irritability, impatience, difficulty concentrating, and mood swings. It is as if the orchestra is out of tune, with each instrument playing in a different key, creating a disharmonious melody.

Insomnia and anxiety: Anxiety and insomnia often feed each other, creating a vicious cycle. Anxiety makes it difficult to sleep, and lack of sleep increases anxiety, generating a constant state of alertness that prevents relaxation and rest.

Sleep and depression: Depression can also affect sleep quality, causing insomnia or excessive sleepiness. The chemical imbalance in the brain that characterizes depression interferes with sleep cycles, affecting the production of hormones such as melatonin and serotonin.

Sleep hygiene: Creating a regular sleep routine, with set times to sleep and wake up, and adopting habits that promote relaxation and sleep, such as a warm bath, relaxing reading, or meditation, is like setting the stage for the presentation of the sleep orchestra.

Environment conducive to sleep: A dark, quiet room with a pleasant temperature is like a cozy auditorium that invites rest and relaxation. Avoid using electronics before bed, as the blue light emitted by these devices can interfere with the production of melatonin, a hormone that regulates sleep. 1

Seeking professional help: If you suffer from chronic insomnia or other sleep disorders, do not hesitate to seek help from a healthcare professional. A sleep specialist can help you identify the causes of the problem and find solutions for a more peaceful and restful night's sleep.

Sleep, in its essence, is an act of surrender that reconnects us with inner harmony. It offers us a necessary pause for the body to regenerate and emotions to settle, preparing us for the rebirth of each day. When we prioritize restful sleep, we create space for the balance between body and mind to flourish.

Recognizing the importance of sleep is honoring a natural cycle that sustains our emotions and cognitive abilities. Small adjustments in the environment, routine, and care for emotional well-being can transform restless nights into moments of true restoration, strengthening our willingness and mental clarity.

Thus, the symphony of rest becomes an indispensable guide to a lighter and fuller life. With each good night's sleep, we reinforce the foundations of our health, allowing the orchestra of body and mind to play in perfect harmony for lasting well-being.

Chapter 40
Technology and Emotions

Technology has established itself as a central element in the contemporary human experience, shaping interactions, learning, and the way we understand the world around us. It is not just a tool that facilitates processes, but also a force capable of transforming lives, bringing people closer, providing access to information, and expanding the frontiers of creativity and innovation. However, technology does not operate in isolation; its influence is intrinsically linked to the emotions it awakens, the connections it fosters, and the challenges it imposes. Thus, understanding the emotional impact of technology is essential to using it in a way that enriches, rather than overwhelms, our lives.

While enabling incredible experiences, technology demands our attention so that we can use it in a balanced way. It is necessary to recognize that constant exposure to digital stimuli can impact our emotional health, influence our way of thinking, and even alter the way we deal with the physical world and interpersonal relationships. Therefore, more than just a set of resources, technology should be seen as a platform that reflects our intentions and choices. Only when we learn to manage this relationship consciously can we direct it towards purposes that promote well-being, genuine connection, and personal growth.

Furthermore, technology carries with it a paradox: it brings us closer and, at the same time, can distance us. The ability to send an instant message to someone on the other side of the world is one of the greatest achievements of our time, but excessive use of screens often distances us from face-to-face interactions and moments of true human connection. It is essential to see technology not as an end in itself, but as a means to expand our capabilities and enrich our experiences, without neglecting the emotions and needs that make us human. Just as a skilled conductor must balance each sound of his orchestra, it is up to us to learn to balance the different aspects of technology in our lives.

The relationship between technology and emotions is a complex and challenging dance in the digital age. Just as technology can connect us with loved ones, inform us, and entertain us, it can also distract us, isolate us, and overload us with information and stimuli. Finding balance in the use of technology is essential to cultivate emotional well-being and build a healthy relationship with the digital world.

Tuning the technological orchestra:

Digital awareness: The first step towards a healthy relationship with technology is to develop digital awareness, that is, the ability to use technology intentionally, responsibly, and aware of its impacts on our lives. It is like the conductor who studies the score before the concert, understanding the structure of the music and the role of each instrument.

Managing screen time: Setting limits on the time spent in front of screens is essential to avoid overstimulation, mental fatigue, and sleep deprivation. It is like the conductor who defines the time of each movement of the symphony, ensuring that the music has rhythm and harmony.

Cultivating real relationships: Prioritizing face-to-face interactions, human contact, and moments of coexistence with loved ones is fundamental to nurture emotional bonds and combat social isolation. It is like the conductor who values the interaction between the musicians, creating an atmosphere of collaboration and harmony in the orchestra.

Protecting privacy: Paying attention to privacy settings on social networks and applications, and sharing personal information carefully and responsibly, is essential to protect your identity and your digital security. It is like the conductor who protects his musicians from distractions and external interference, allowing them to concentrate on the music.

Filtering content: Being selective with the information you consume on social networks and the internet, and avoiding excessive negative news and toxic content, is essential to protect your mental health and cultivate positive emotions. It is like the conductor who chooses the best scores for his orchestra, selecting music that inspires, elevates, and touches the soul.

Disconnecting to connect: Setting aside moments of the day to disconnect from the digital world, practice outdoor activities, meditate, or simply relax in silence, is essential to recharge your batteries, calm your mind, and reconnect with yourself. It is like the conductor who grants an interval to the musicians, allowing them to rest and prepare for the next stage of the concert.

Seeking professional support: If you feel that the use of technology is negatively affecting your life, your relationships, or your mental health, do not hesitate to seek professional help. A therapist or psychologist can help you identify problematic behavior patterns and develop strategies for a healthier relationship with technology.

Technology, when used with balance and intention, can be a powerful ally in building a more connected and emotionally enriched world. However, recognizing its impacts and limitations is essential to maintain control over how it influences our minds and our relationships.

By creating spaces for conscious disconnection, we prioritize moments of genuine presence that reinforce human bonds and cultivate well-being. Thus, technology is transformed from a source of distraction to a tool that enhances our experiences and supports our emotional growth.

Understanding and adjusting this relationship is like tuning an instrument in a large orchestra: each conscious choice contributes to a harmonious melody, in which the balance between the digital and the human creates a fuller, more connected, and meaningful life.

Chapter 41
The Art of Adaptation

Life is a constant flow, like a river that crosses varied landscapes, challenging us to understand and master its dynamics to move forward with purpose and balance. Each change represents a moment of inevitable transformation, capable of redefining the trajectory of our choices and taking us out of the comfort of the predictable. Like a canoeist in the midst of rapids, we are invited to face adversity with courage, adjusting our movements to the force of the circumstances that surround us. This ability to adapt is not just a reaction; it is a refined art that combines acceptance, flexibility, and resilience, allowing us to transform challenges into opportunities for personal growth and renewal.

Accepting mutability as a constant is the first step to navigating the uncertain waters of existence. By recognizing that life is in constant transformation, we learn to abandon unproductive resistance and embrace the new as a learning opportunity. However, accepting does not mean resigning oneself; it implies observing each change clearly and seeking ways to act proactively. This attitude is essential to keep an open mind and explore paths that help us grow, even when we are confronted with unexpected twists and turns.

Furthermore, flexibility becomes an indispensable tool to adjust course when the unexpected alters the landscape. Facing change requires the ability to reinterpret challenges and reformulate our strategies to move forward. It is in this context that resilience shines as an indispensable quality, ensuring that after each fall, there is strength to start over. Allied to these virtues, optimism acts as a compass, pointing to the possibilities that arise in each situation, illuminating the path with hope and purpose. With self-knowledge, planning, and social support, we can transform the art of adaptation into a safe guide to face any current that life presents us.

Changes are inevitable, a constant in a permanently transforming universe. They can be planned, such as a change of house or job, or unexpected, such as a loss, an illness, or a global crisis. Regardless of their nature, changes take us out of our comfort zone, challenge us to reassess our beliefs and values, and drive us to grow and adapt.

Navigating the rapids of life:

Acceptance: The first step in dealing with change is to accept it as a natural part of life. Resisting change is like paddling against the current, expending energy and getting frustrated unnecessarily. Accepting change is like letting yourself be carried by the current, trusting the strength of the river and adapting to its flow.

Flexibility: Flexibility is the ability to adapt to new circumstances, to change direction when necessary, and to find creative solutions to the challenges that arise. It is like the canoeist who uses the paddle to maneuver the boat, circumventing obstacles and following the course of the river.

Resilience: Resilience is the ability to recover from adversity, to learn from difficult experiences, and to move forward with strength and optimism. It is like the canoeist who, after falling into the water, gets up, gets back in the boat, and continues paddling with determination.

Optimism: Maintaining a positive perspective in the face of change, focusing on the opportunities and possibilities that they bring, is like having a beacon that illuminates the path, guiding us through the darkness.

Self-knowledge: Understanding your own emotions, your limits, and your needs is essential to navigate changes with more awareness and balance. It is like knowing your own boat, its capabilities and its limits, so that you can navigate safely.

Planning: When change is planned, planning is like a map that guides us towards our destination, helping us to prepare for challenges and organize the necessary resources.

Social support: Having the support of loved ones, sharing your feelings and seeking help when needed is like having a support team that helps us navigate, giving us strength and security to face the rapids.

The art of adaptation is, above all, a celebration of our ability to evolve in the face of life's inevitable changes. Each challenge faced with acceptance and flexibility strengthens our abilities to flow with circumstances, transforming uncertainties into new beginnings and opportunities.

By developing resilience and cultivating optimism, we learn to face the unexpected as an invitation to grow and rediscover our potential. In this process, self-knowledge and the support of those we love become indispensable compasses, guiding us with clarity and confidence.

Thus, we navigate the unpredictable waters of existence, not as victims of the currents, but as masters of our course, steering the ship of life with courage, purpose, and the art of transforming each change into a step towards full realization.

Chapter 42
The Compass of Emotional Intelligence

Life is a journey full of decisions that shape our path, and emotional intelligence is the essential instrument that guides us through this complexity. Each choice we make is an opportunity to align our actions with our values, overcome challenges, and find meaning in our journey. By understanding the fundamental role of emotions in our decisions, we become more aware and effective navigators, capable of building a life consistent with our goals and aspirations.

Emotional intelligence acts as an internal navigation system, allowing us to interpret the signals of emotions and use them as tools of discernment. It not only helps us understand how we feel about a choice, but also to assess how our emotions influence our perceptions and priorities. Through this ability, we transform decision-making into a process that balances logic and intuition, rationality and sensitivity.

More than just a resource, emotional intelligence enables us to recognize our fears, doubts, and uncertainties without allowing them to dominate our trajectory. It promotes the self-confidence necessary to face difficult choices and the flexibility to adjust our course as challenges arise. This combination of self-knowledge, conscious analysis, and emotional management is what allows us to navigate complex scenarios with clarity and determination, keeping us connected to our true purposes.

Making decisions is an art that requires not only rationality and logic, but also the ability to understand and manage emotions. Emotions influence our perceptions, shape our priorities, and propel us towards certain choices. Emotional intelligence allows us to use emotions as allies in the decision-making process, helping us to make more conscious, balanced, and authentic choices.

Mapping the path of decisions:

Self-knowledge: The first step to making more conscious decisions is to know yourself deeply, understanding your values, your needs, your desires, and your life goals. It is like identifying the starting point on the map, the place from which you are starting and where you want to go.

Clarity and focus: Clearly define what you want to achieve with your decision, what your goals are, and what are the most important criteria to be considered. It is like plotting the route on the map, defining the destination and the landmarks along the way.

Rational analysis: Evaluate the different options, weigh the pros and cons of each, and seek relevant information that can help you make a more informed choice. It is like studying the map carefully, identifying the different paths, the obstacles, and the available resources.

Intuition and emotions: Pay attention to your intuition, your feelings, and the sensations that each option causes you. Emotions can give us valuable clues about which path is most aligned with our values and our deepest needs. It is like feeling the direction of the wind, which can guide us through the fog.

Fear management: Fear can paralyze us in the face of important decisions, preventing us from taking risks and moving forward. Recognize your fears, but don't let them dominate you. Remember that courage is not the absence of fear, but the ability to act despite it.

Confidence and self-efficacy: Believe in your ability to make the right choice, to deal with the consequences of your decision, and to learn from your mistakes. Self-confidence is like the rudder of the ship, which keeps us on the right course, even in the midst of storms.

Flexibility and adaptation: Things don't always go as planned. Be open to changing direction, reassessing your choices, and adapting to new circumstances. Flexibility is like the sail of the ship, which adjusts to the direction of the wind, propelling us towards our destination.

Emotional intelligence is the compass that keeps us aligned with our values and purposes as we navigate the complexities of life. It teaches us that each decision carries not only a rational choice, but also an emotional resonance that needs to be embraced and understood.

By integrating self-knowledge, intuition, and conscious analysis, we acquire the ability to act with clarity, even in the face of uncertainty. This practice not only strengthens our decision-making ability, but also allows us to create more authentic and meaningful paths in our journey.

With emotional intelligence as a guide, we learn to adjust our sails, face storms, and take advantage of favorable winds. Thus, we move forward, building a trajectory that reflects not only who we are, but also who we want to become, with confidence, balance, and determination.

Chapter 43
Aligning Emotions with Goals

Life can be understood as a carefully planned journey, where each decision we make sets the course that leads us to achieve our dreams and goals. In this scenario, goals play the role of a clear roadmap, pointing us in the right direction, while emotions act as the driving force that fuels our progress. Establishing a harmonious connection between emotions and goals is what makes the journey towards our purposes a more fluid and efficient experience. Just as a sailor adjusts the sails to take advantage of a tailwind, aligning emotions with goals allows us to move forward in a more balanced way, aligned with what truly matters.

Recognizing the importance of emotions in the pursuit of goals is fundamental to achieving consistent and satisfying results. They are not mere impulses or momentary reactions, but powerful indicators of our deepest desires and values. When we use our emotions as allies in the goal-setting process, we strengthen our ability to stay focused and motivated, even in the face of inevitable challenges and changes. In this way, we manage to transform potential obstacles into opportunities for learning and personal growth, without losing sight of the defined direction.

By integrating emotion and reason into our goal planning, we create a solid foundation for more conscious and effective decisions. This means recognizing that each step towards our goals must reflect not only what we want to achieve, but also who we are and what moves us internally. This approach allows for a healthier relationship with the process, promoting self-knowledge and increasing the chances of perseverance along the way. The journey, then, ceases to be just a relentless pursuit of results and becomes an enriching experience in itself.

Finally, aligning emotions and goals is an invitation to live more authentically and fully. This alignment does not eliminate challenges, but prepares us to face them with resilience and confidence, knowing that we are navigating with purpose and clarity. Just as a sailor relies on the balance between wind, tide, and direction to reach their destination, those who adjust their emotions to harmonize with their goals discover a renewable source of energy and inspiration. This integration is the key to turning dreams into reality and building a path of genuine and meaningful achievements.

Setting goals is an essential process to give direction and purpose to life. Clear and well-defined goals motivate us to act, to overcome obstacles, and to persist in our efforts. However, setting goals is not enough. It is necessary that these goals are aligned with our emotions, with our values, and with our deepest desires. When there is this harmony between reason and emotion, the journey becomes more enjoyable, meaningful, and fulfilling.

Charting the course of life:

Dreams and aspirations: The starting point for setting goals is to connect with your dreams and aspirations, with what really matters to you. It's like choosing the destination of the trip, the place you long to know and explore.

Values and purposes: The goals we set must be aligned with our values and life purposes, with what gives us meaning and direction. It's like choosing the type of ship that will take you to your destination, the one that represents your ideals and beliefs.

SMART goals: Goals must be specific, measurable, achievable, relevant, and time-bound. This methodology, known as SMART, helps us define clearer, more objective, and realistic goals. It's like accurately plotting the route on the map, defining the coordinates, the distance to be covered, and the estimated time of arrival.

Visualization: Visualizing yourself achieving your goals, experiencing the positive emotions and benefits they will bring, is like feeling the wind blowing in the sails, propelling the ship towards its destination. Creative visualization is a powerful tool for strengthening motivation and confidence.

Planning and action: Setting goals without acting is like having a map without leaving the place. It is necessary to draw up an action plan, define the steps to be followed, and commit to carrying out the necessary tasks. It's like weighing anchor, hoisting the sails, and starting to sail towards the horizon.

Flexibility and adaptation: The path is not always linear and predictable. Be prepared to change course, reassess your goals, and adapt to new circumstances. Flexibility is like the navigator's ability to adjust the ship's sails to changes in the wind, maintaining course towards the destination.

Celebration and recognition: Recognizing and celebrating each milestone reached, each obstacle overcome, and each goal achieved is like having a party on board the ship, recognizing the effort and dedication of the crew. Celebration renews energy and strengthens motivation to continue the journey.

Aligning emotions with goals is a journey that unites reason and heart in an authentic and transformative trajectory. This balance allows us to move forward with clarity, nurturing a deep connection between our dreams and the actions that lead us to them. By listening to our emotions, we discover genuine motivations that make each step more meaningful and rewarding.

By integrating personal values, strategic planning, and the ability to adapt, we create a path that reflects who we truly are. Resilience and flexibility make us skilled navigators, capable of adjusting course without losing sight of our destination, even amidst the unpredictable winds of life.

With this alignment, the pursuit of goals ceases to be just a goal to be achieved and becomes an experience of growth and celebration. With each achievement, we reaffirm our purpose, renew our energies, and strengthen the certainty that, with reason and emotion in harmony, the horizon of our dreams is always within our reach.

Chapter 44
Overcoming Trauma

A trauma can be described as a deep mark on the soul, an experience that challenges our ability to cope with adversity and leaves traces in the form of emotional and psychological pain. Overcoming trauma is not just a desire, but a need to restore inner balance, rediscover inner strength, and regain control over one's own life. Facing trauma requires courage and a commitment to self-healing, a process that involves not only acknowledging the pain but transforming it into learning and growth. This journey, although challenging, is the key to reframing our experiences and building a more resilient and meaningful life.

Psychological traumas often emerge from unexpected and overwhelming events, such as accidents, violence, irreparable losses, or natural disasters, which directly threaten our physical or emotional integrity. These experiences can trigger intense responses, such as fear, helplessness, and isolation, that persist even after the traumatic event has ended. The consequences are varied and can include symptoms such as constant anxiety, difficulty sleeping, intrusive thoughts, or even challenges in establishing healthy interpersonal relationships. However, recognizing these manifestations as parts of a natural process is essential to begin the journey towards healing and emotional freedom.

Overcoming trauma is not about forgetting or erasing the past, but about building new meanings and opening paths to a lighter and fuller life. This involves seeking professional support, adopting self-care practices, and investing in therapeutic strategies that help process difficult memories. Thus, by engaging with this process, the pain of trauma can be transformed into a powerful tool for self-discovery and personal empowerment. No matter how long and challenging the journey may seem, it carries with it the promise of a future full of possibilities and a reunion with inner peace.

A psychological trauma is an intense emotional response to an overwhelming event that threatens our physical or emotional integrity. Accidents, violence, abuse, significant losses, natural disasters – these are some examples of events that can cause psychological trauma. The wounds of trauma can manifest themselves in many ways, such as anxiety, depression, insomnia, nightmares, flashbacks, difficulty concentrating, and relationship problems.

Treading the path of healing:

Recognize and accept the trauma: The first step to overcoming trauma is to recognize it and accept it as part of your history. Denying or repressing the pain of trauma is like trying to hide an open wound, preventing it from healing. Recognizing the trauma is like cleaning the wound, allowing the healing process to begin.

Seek professional support: Overcoming trauma can be a challenging process, and seeking help from a mental health professional is essential to receive the necessary support and guidance. A qualified therapist can offer you a safe space to explore your emotions, understand the impacts of trauma, and develop coping strategies.

Therapeutic techniques: There are several therapeutic approaches that can help in overcoming trauma, such as cognitive behavioral therapy (CBT), EMDR therapy (Eye Movement Desensitization and Reprocessing), and somatic therapy. These therapies use specific techniques to process traumatic memories, reduce the symptoms of anxiety and post-traumatic stress, and promote emotional regulation.

Self-care: Taking care of yourself is essential during the trauma healing process. Prioritize healthy habits, such as a balanced diet, regular exercise, adequate sleep, and contact with nature. Make time for activities that bring you pleasure and relaxation, such as reading, music, contact with friends and family.

Self-compassion: Be kind and understanding to yourself during this journey. Recognize that you are going through a difficult time and that it is natural to feel pain, fear, and insecurity. Treat yourself with the same compassion and care that you would offer a dear friend.

Reframing: Overcoming trauma can be an opportunity to reframe the painful experience, finding lessons and transforming pain into strength and resilience. It's like turning the wound into a scar that tells a story of overcoming and courage.

Reconstruction: After the healing process, it is time to rebuild your life based on new, stronger and more resilient foundations. Set new goals, pursue new dreams, cultivate healthy relationships, and embrace life with renewed hope and confidence.

Overcoming trauma is an act of courage and renewal, a journey that transforms deep wounds into milestones of overcoming and strength. Recognizing pain and seeking support are fundamental steps to open space for healing, allowing difficult memories to become lessons and intense emotions to find balance.

As the process of self-compassion and self-care develops, trauma ceases to be an oppressive shadow and becomes a part of personal history that makes us more resilient and aware of our power of transformation. This reframing is an invitation to discover new meanings in life and build a healthier relationship with yourself and others.

Each step on the path of healing is a reminder that, even in the face of the most challenging adversities, it is possible to find inner peace and create a future full of possibilities, guided by the inner strength that flourishes in the heart of those who choose to move on.

Chapter 45
Dealing with Loss

Dealing with loss is an experience that involves facing the abrupt interruption of something or someone that has profoundly marked our existence. Like a storm that devastates the garden of life, loss confronts us with the destruction of what we knew and valued, requiring us to deal with the emotional and spiritual wreckage left behind. However, more than a moment of suffering, this experience marks the beginning of a complex and transformative process, where the pain of absence is reframed into memory, learning, and reconstruction. This journey is an essential part of the human condition, being both a challenge and an opportunity for self-discovery and growth.

Loss manifests itself in different ways – be it through the death of a loved one, the dissolution of a relationship, the loss of a job, a dream, or even an important phase of life. Regardless of its nature, it forces us to re-evaluate our perception of stability and security, challenging us to find meaning in absence. This process requires a deep dive into our emotions, where grief acts as a safe space to express what we feel and begin to understand the impact of what is gone. It is not just about overcoming, but about integrating loss as part of our history, recognizing its role in shaping who we are.

As we walk through the valley of grief, we are called to cultivate a balance between accepting irreversible reality and rebuilding our lives with new meanings. This path requires self-compassion, patience, and courage to embrace memories and longing without being paralyzed by them. Honoring what has been lost, whether through rituals, memories, or actions that keep its essence alive, is a way of transforming pain into a force for renewal. Thus, the process of dealing with loss is not just an act of resistance, but also a journey of recreation, where, little by little, the devastated garden begins to bloom again.

Loss is a universal experience, an inevitable part of life. We can lose loved ones, relationships, jobs, material possessions, health, dreams, youth. Each loss leaves a mark on our history, a scar that reminds us of the fragility of life and the importance of valuing each moment.

Crossing the valley of grief:

Allow yourself to feel the pain: Denying or repressing the pain of loss is like trying to contain the storm, preventing it from following its natural course. Allowing yourself to feel the pain, cry, mourn, express your sadness and longing is like letting the rain fall, washing the soul and clearing the ground for renewal.

Respect your time: The grieving process is unique to each person and there is no set time for it to be completed. Respect your own pace, without comparing yourself to others or charging yourself to "get over" the loss quickly. It's like waiting for the soil to dry naturally after the rain, without forcing the process.

Take care of yourself: In the midst of the pain of loss, it is essential to prioritize self-care. Eat healthily, exercise regularly, get enough sleep, and make time for activities that bring you comfort and relaxation. It's like nourishing the plants in the garden with water and light, helping them recover from the storm.

Honor the memory: Finding ways to honor the memory of what has been lost can bring comfort and help in the healing process. Creating a memorial, writing a farewell letter, sharing stories and memories with loved ones are ways to keep the connection with what is gone alive. It's like planting a new flower in the garden, in honor of the one that was lost.

Accept the new reality: Loss forces us to accept a new reality, a world without the presence of what is gone. This acceptance does not mean forgetting or ceasing to love, but rather finding a way to move on, integrating loss into your history and building a new chapter in your life. It's like redesigning the garden, creating a new landscape that honors the past and embraces the future.

Seek social support: Sharing your pain with loved ones, seeking support groups, or seeking help from a mental health professional can provide you with the comfort, understanding, and support you need to get through the grieving process. It's like getting help from other gardeners to rebuild the garden after the storm.

Find a new purpose: Loss can lead us to question the meaning of life and seek new purposes and motivations. Finding new passions, dedicating yourself to social causes, helping others, or connecting with spirituality can bring new meaning to life and help you rediscover joy and hope. It's like discovering new seeds to plant in the garden, cultivating life with renewed enthusiasm.

Dealing with loss is a process that requires surrender and courage, an invitation to honor what is gone while building something new. Allowing yourself to experience pain is essential, as each tear shed is part of the path that leads us to acceptance and rediscovering our inner strength.

By integrating memories with new meanings, we cultivate fertile ground for the blossoming of new hopes. With patience and care, we begin to see beyond the storm, realizing that the essence of what we love remains alive in our actions, memories, and transformations.

This journey of reconstruction teaches us that, even in the face of absence, it is possible to rediscover joy and purpose. In the garden of life, the flowers we lose make way for new seeds, renewing the cycle of existence and strengthening our ability to move forward with courage and love.

Chapter 46
Acceptance:
Embracing Reality with Serenity

Acceptance is the ability to welcome life as it presents itself, without resistance or judgment, allowing each experience, emotion, or thought to flow naturally. It does not require resignation, but rather a conscious act of acknowledging and integrating reality, understanding that the universe follows its course with or without our intervention. Like a river that flows through mountains and valleys, acceptance invites us to observe and fully experience each moment, understanding that change and impermanence are part of existence. Resistance, in turn, becomes the weight that prevents us from enjoying the lightness of life's flow.

Accepting reality is an exercise in courage and wisdom, an invitation to relate to our emotions and thoughts in a more compassionate way. This process begins when we abandon the struggle against what we cannot change, recognizing circumstances as they are. It does not mean giving up or settling, but rather realizing that by accepting, we free up energy to transform what is within our reach and to deal with what is beyond our control. Acceptance connects us to the present, allowing us to recognize the beauties and challenges of each moment as part of a larger, harmonious whole.

In practice, acceptance involves a kind look at our imperfections, understanding that they do not define us, but enrich our journey. It is an act of profound self-acceptance and self-love, while at the same time expanding our compassion for others and the world around us. It is allowing the ups and downs of life to coexist, as the necessary contrast for us to fully appreciate the beauty of existence. By accepting, we find serenity even in adversity, and we discover that inner peace is not in the absence of challenges, but in how we relate to them.

Acceptance is not passivity or resignation. It is a conscious choice to embrace reality as it is, with its ups and downs, its joys and sorrows, its successes and mistakes. It is recognizing that life is a constant flow of change, and that resistance to this flow only generates tension and suffering.

Finding peace in acceptance:

Accepting emotions: Acceptance begins with accepting one's own emotions, whether they are pleasant or unpleasant. It is allowing yourself to feel joy, sadness, anger, fear, without judgment or resistance. It is like watching the waves of the sea, letting them come and go without trying to control them.

Accepting thoughts: Just like emotions, thoughts also come and go, like clouds passing through the sky of the mind. Accepting thoughts is observing them without identifying with them, without being carried away by them. It is like watching the clouds go by without trying to grab them or push them away.

Accepting imperfections: Acceptance implies recognizing and accepting one's own imperfections, limits, and weaknesses. It is abandoning the search for perfection and loving yourself as you are, with your flaws and qualities. It is like accepting the stones in the river's path, recognizing that they are part of the landscape.

Accepting the present: Accepting the present is living in the here and now, without dwelling on the past or worrying about the future. It is appreciating the beauty of the present moment, with its challenges and opportunities. It is like bathing in the waters of the river, feeling its temperature, its movement, its energy.

Accepting change: Change is the only constant in life. Accepting change is adapting to the flow of life, letting go of what no longer serves us, and embracing the new with courage and curiosity. It is like following the course of the river, trusting that it will lead you to new horizons.

Accepting uncertainty: Life is full of uncertainties, and trying to control everything is an illusion. Accepting uncertainty is trusting in the wisdom of life, surrendering to the flow of the universe, and accepting that not everything is under our control. It is like navigating the river without knowing exactly what lies ahead, but trusting that the current will take you to a good place.

Acceptance and spirituality: For many people, acceptance is deeply connected to spirituality. Belief in a higher power, a greater purpose, or a cosmic order can bring comfort and acceptance in the face of life's difficulties. It is like feeling part of something bigger, trusting that the river of life flows into an ocean of love and wisdom.

Acceptance is the key that opens the doors to a lighter and more meaningful existence. By embracing reality as it is, without resistance or judgment, we free ourselves from the emotional burden of fighting the uncontrollable. This conscious surrender connects us to the present moment, where true serenity resides.

Accepting changes, ups and downs, and uncertainties is recognizing that we are part of a continuous flow, where each experience, whether challenging or enriching, contributes to our growth. In this movement, we learn that inner peace is born from harmony with reality and not from its denial.

This practice teaches us to walk through life with more compassion for ourselves and others, transforming challenges into learning and imperfections into beauty. Thus, the act of accepting is not a renunciation, but a celebration of what it means to be fully alive, flowing like the river that always finds its way.

Chapter 47
Exploring the Depths of the Psyche

The human mind can be understood as a vast and complex system, where only a small part is accessible to conscious perception. The thoughts and emotions that we identify in everyday life form the surface of a much deeper structure, full of memories, beliefs, and emotions that operate silently in the unconscious. The exploration of this hidden territory is not just an introspective journey; it is an opportunity to reveal the roots of behavior patterns, overcome internal barriers, and access the wealth of resources that shape the essence of who we are. This journey of self-discovery is both challenging and transformative, allowing us to access unexplored layers of our psyche to promote growth and freedom.

The process of deep self-knowledge requires courage to confront the unknown. As we dive into the vastness of the unconscious, we encounter repressed content that may be influencing our decisions and emotions. These discoveries, sometimes uncomfortable, are fundamental to transformation. Identifying the patterns that govern our actions and recognizing limiting beliefs offers us a clear vision of what has been preventing us from reaching our potential. This understanding not only illuminates the path to personal growth but also prepares us to deal more consciously and assertively with life's challenges.

More than a simple exercise in introspection, exploring the human mind involves recognizing that it is composed of archetypal and symbolic dimensions. Archetypes, as universal figures of wisdom and transformation, help us understand the roles we play and the challenges we face. Symbols, by translating the mysteries of the unconscious into understandable forms, become indispensable guides on this journey. The integration of our shadows - the aspects that we reject or deny in ourselves - is an essential step to achieve a state of balance. When we embrace these parts of our psyche, we discover the ability to transform vulnerabilities into strengths and fears into learning.

Thus, the exploration of the depths of the psyche is not just a search for answers, but a journey towards freedom and fulfillment. By connecting with the deepest aspects of our mind, we acquire tools to redesign our present and build a future aligned with our essence.

Deep self-knowledge goes beyond simply identifying superficial emotions and thoughts. It is a search for understanding our essence, our history, the forces that motivate us, and the fears that limit us. It is a journey of self-discovery that allows us to unravel the labyrinth of our mind and free ourselves from the shackles of the past.

Diving into the depths:

Exploration of the unconscious: The unconscious is a reservoir of memories, emotions, beliefs, and experiences that influence our behavior without our being aware of them. Through techniques such as psychoanalysis, hypnosis, and meditation, we can access the unconscious and bring to the surface repressed content that may be blocking our growth and happiness.

Identifying patterns: We often repeat dysfunctional behavior patterns without realizing it, as if we were stuck in a vicious cycle. Deep self-knowledge allows us to identify these patterns, understand their origins, and develop strategies to break them.

Limiting beliefs: Limiting beliefs are like chains that bind us to the past, preventing us from reaching our potential. Deep self-knowledge allows us to identify these beliefs, question them, and replace them with more empowering beliefs.

Inner shadow: We all have an inner shadow, a part of us that we reject or hide, composed of aspects that we consider negative or unacceptable. Integrating the shadow is accepting these parts of ourselves, understanding them, and transforming them into positive forces.

Archetypes and symbols: Archetypes are universal patterns of behavior and experience that manifest themselves in our psyche, such as the hero, the mother, the wise man, the shadow. Symbols are images and metaphors that represent these archetypes and connect us with deeper dimensions of our being. Understanding the archetypes and symbols that inhabit us is like unraveling the language of the unconscious, accessing the ancestral wisdom that resides within us.

Hero's journey: The hero's journey is a metaphor for the process of self-knowledge and personal transformation. Just as the hero faces challenges, overcomes obstacles, and returns transformed from his journey, we too can venture on an inner journey of self-discovery, facing our fears, healing our wounds, and awakening our maximum potential.

Exploring the depths of the psyche is embarking on an intimate and transformative journey, where each discovery brings us closer to our essence. As we unravel the mysteries of the unconscious, we gain the clarity necessary to understand patterns, integrate our shadows, and access inner resources that previously seemed out of reach.

This quest is not linear, but rich in learning. By recognizing and accepting both our strengths and our vulnerabilities, we open the way for a more genuine connection with ourselves. In this process, archetypes and symbols become precious allies, translating the incomprehensible into insights that illuminate our journey.

The dive into the psyche not only reveals who we are, but also who we can become. It is a journey of self-discovery and empowerment, where the depths of our mind are transformed into a vast ocean of possibilities, guiding us towards freedom and complete fulfillment.

Chapter 48
Social Intelligence

Society functions as an intricate network of human relationships, where each individual plays a unique role, linked to others by invisible threads of interaction and mutual dependence. Social intelligence is the ability to understand these connections and act with skill and sensitivity, strengthening bonds, promoting mutual understanding, and contributing to collective well-being. More than a simple aptitude, it represents a sophisticated set of skills that make it possible to interpret social dynamics, build healthy relationships, and create a positive impact both in small circles and in wider communities.

This ability goes beyond polite behavior or effective communication; it is about seeing relationships as a whole, identifying patterns and needs that are often implicit. By developing social intelligence, a person becomes able to decipher emotional and social nuances, transforming everyday interactions into opportunities to deepen bonds and resolve conflicts. It is like strengthening a web of relationships, where each thread represents trust, empathy, and collaboration, creating a more robust and resilient structure.

By applying social intelligence in our daily lives, we promote an environment of mutual respect and joint growth. Understanding others' emotions and acting with compassion allows us to build solid bridges between people, while clear and assertive communication facilitates understanding and resolves differences peacefully. This network of skills not only helps us to face interpersonal challenges, but also positions us as agents of social transformation, ready to inspire and lead with ethics, empathy, and purpose.

Social intelligence goes beyond basic social skills such as communication and empathy. It is a combination of skills that allow us to understand social dynamics, build healthy relationships, resolve conflicts constructively, and contribute to a more just and compassionate world.

Weaving the web of relationships:

Social understanding: Social intelligence begins with the ability to understand human behavior, emotions, motivations, and social interactions. It is like observing the web carefully, identifying the different types of threads, their textures, and their connections.

Empathy and compassion: Putting yourself in another's shoes, understanding their feelings and perspectives, and showing compassion and solidarity are essential skills for building authentic and meaningful relationships. It is like choosing the softest and most resistant threads to weave the web, those that provide comfort and support.

Effective communication: Communicating clearly, assertively, and respectfully, expressing your ideas, needs, and emotions constructively, is fundamental to establishing genuine connections and resolving conflicts peacefully. It is like using a common language that allows all the nodes in the web to understand and connect with each other.

Cooperation and collaboration: Working as a team, sharing responsibilities, respecting differences, and seeking solutions together is essential to the success of any group or community. It is like joining forces to build a stronger and more resilient web, capable of withstanding winds and storms.

Inspirational leadership: Leaders with social intelligence inspire, motivate, and guide their followers with vision, empathy, and ethics. They create an environment of trust and collaboration, where each individual feels valued and motivated to contribute to the common good. It is like being the central point of the web, radiating energy and directing the flow of relationships.

Conflict resolution: Conflicts are inevitable in human relationships, but how we deal with them can strengthen or weaken bonds. Social intelligence allows us to face conflicts calmly, respectfully, and with a search for solutions that benefit everyone involved. It is like repairing damage to the web, rebuilding connections with more strength and resilience.

Community building: Social intelligence drives us to contribute to the well-being of the community, to promote social justice, and to build a more harmonious and sustainable world. It is like expanding the web, creating new connections and strengthening the bonds between individuals.

Social intelligence is the foundation of a richer, more harmonious, and meaningful human coexistence. It enables us to see beyond words and actions, interpreting the emotions, intentions, and needs that shape interactions. By cultivating it, we transform our relationships into sources of mutual learning and collective construction.

This skill teaches us that each thread of the social network we weave is essential, and that acts of empathy, compassion, and sincere communication have the power to strengthen human connections. Through it, we are able to resolve conflicts with respect, lead with integrity, and create environments where everyone feels valued.

By applying social intelligence, we amplify our impact on the world, helping to weave a more just, collaborative, and welcoming society. In this process, we discover that true power lies in our connections and in the ability to transform each interaction into an opportunity for growth and harmony.

Chapter 49
Leadership and Emotional Management

A leader is the essence that guides teams and organizations through uncertainties and challenges, offering direction, purpose, and inspiration. Leadership is not just about guiding; it's about creating an environment of trust and growth, where people feel valued and motivated to achieve their best. For this, emotional management becomes an indispensable component, acting as the stabilizing force that allows the leader to face pressures, understand the emotions of others, and act with balance in any circumstance.

Emotional management, integrated with leadership, is more than just controlling reactions; it is a skill that combines self-awareness, empathy, and emotional intelligence to build genuine connections. Leaders who master this competence not only deal with challenges but also transform obstacles into opportunities for learning and progress. They demonstrate a presence that inspires confidence while maintaining the clarity needed to make decisions in critical moments.

At its core, leadership with emotional management goes beyond leading with the mind: it incorporates the heart. This means that, when leading, it is essential to understand the motivations and needs of others, promote an environment of mutual support, and communicate with purpose. This approach creates a solid foundation for collective success, making the leader not just a guide, but a source of stability and hope even in the most turbulent times.

Leadership and emotional management complement each other like two sides of the same coin. A leader who masters the art of emotional management can connect with their followers on a deeper level, inspiring them to do their best, overcome challenges, and achieve extraordinary results. It is the leader who guides with the heart, with empathy, compassion, and emotional intelligence.

Illuminating the path of leadership:

Self-awareness: The leader who knows himself deeply, who understands his strengths, weaknesses, values, and purposes, has a solid foundation to lead with authenticity and confidence. It is like the lighthouse that knows its own structure, its limits, and its capabilities, and that stands firm even in the midst of storms.

Empathy: Empathy is the ability to put yourself in another's shoes, to understand their feelings, needs, and perspectives. An empathetic leader can create genuine connections with their followers, inspiring trust, loyalty, and collaboration. It is like the lighthouse that emits its light in all directions, guiding ships approaching from different points on the horizon.

Inspiring communication: Communication is a leader's most powerful tool. A leader who communicates with clarity, passion, and purpose can inspire, motivate, and mobilize their followers toward a common goal. It is like the lighthouse that emits clear and precise signals, guiding ships through the darkness.

Emotional intelligence: Emotional intelligence is the ability to understand and manage emotions, both your own and those of 1 others. A leader with emotional intelligence can create a climate of trust, respect, and collaboration, where people feel comfortable expressing their ideas, sharing their feelings, and working as a team. It is like the lighthouse that keeps its light on even in the midst of storms, offering safety and stability to ships sailing nearby.

Motivation: A motivating leader can awaken the enthusiasm, passion, and commitment of their followers, inspiring them to do their best and strive for excellence. It is like the lighthouse that guides ships towards safe and prosperous ports, where they can replenish their energies and prepare for new journeys.

Resilience: Resilience is the ability to recover from adversity, learn from mistakes, and move forward with strength and optimism. A resilient leader is an example of overcoming for their followers, showing that it is possible to face challenges and emerge stronger from difficulties. It is like the lighthouse that resists strong winds and giant waves, standing firm and illuminating the path even in the most adverse conditions.

Vision and purpose: A leader with vision and purpose can inspire their followers with a promising future, showing them the way forward and giving them a sense of direction. It is like the lighthouse that guides ships towards a great destination, a place where they can fulfill their dreams and contribute to a better world.

Leading with emotional management is illuminating paths in the midst of uncertainty, offering not only direction but also stability and inspiration. A leader who integrates self-awareness, empathy, and emotional intelligence becomes an anchor for their team, helping them face challenges with confidence and resilience.

This approach transforms leadership into an act of human connection. By listening with empathy, communicating clearly, and leading by example, the leader creates an environment where each individual's potential can flourish. More than results, he cultivates a sense of belonging and purpose that strengthens both the group and its goals.

Thus, leadership with emotional management is not just a practical skill, but a commitment to mutual growth. It is the light that guides teams and organizations beyond storms, always towards safer, more promising ports full of possibilities.

Chapter 50
Emotional Management in the Modern World

The contemporary world is a fast-paced and multifaceted environment, marked by constant innovations, an endless flow of information, and increasing challenges to our emotional health. In this context, emotional management emerges as an indispensable skill, enabling us to face the ups and downs of modern life with resilience and balance. It acts as an internal guide, helping us maintain focus amidst a flood of stimuli, promoting conscious choices aligned with our deepest values.

In the face of an increasingly connected and demanding routine, the ability to manage emotions goes beyond merely alleviating momentary stress. It involves developing a profound awareness of our feelings, identifying emotional triggers, and cultivating practices that promote mental well-being. This skill aids in setting healthy boundaries with technology, avoiding the emotional exhaustion caused by information overload, and fostering a more balanced relationship with the digital and social environment in which we live.

Adopting emotional management in daily life is an essential step in tackling the challenges of modernity.

It helps us find purpose amidst instability, prioritize authentic relationships, and cultivate habits that sustain mental and emotional health. In this way, even in the frenetic pace of the current world, we can create a space for balance and self-care, becoming protagonists of a more conscious, connected, and meaningful life.

The modern world presents a series of unprecedented challenges to our emotional health. The acceleration of life's pace, the overload of information, constant digital connectivity, fierce competitiveness, and future uncertainties can trigger a constant state of alert, posing risks of anxiety, chronic stress, and emotional burnout. Emotional management, therefore, becomes an indispensable tool for navigating this complex territory and building a more balanced, healthy, and meaningful life.

Navigating the challenges of the digital age: The first step toward emotional management in the modern world is developing awareness of one's emotions and the impact of technology on our well-being. It is akin to observing a city map attentively, identifying risk points, congested areas, and the smoothest routes.

Managing information overload: The internet and social media bombard us with a relentless torrent of information, news, and visual stimuli. Learning to filter content, select reliable sources, and disconnect when necessary is essential to protect mental health and avoid burnout. It is like choosing the best routes to bypass chaotic traffic and reach your destination more quickly and calmly.

Cultivating mindfulness: In a world filled with distractions, mindfulness becomes a refuge of peace and concentration. Practicing meditation, conscious breathing, and other mindfulness techniques helps calm the mind, reduce stress, and fully experience the present moment. It is like finding an oasis of peace amidst the hustle and bustle of the metropolis—a place to recharge and reconnect with oneself.

Building meaningful relationships: In an increasingly individualistic and virtual world, cultivating real relationships based on human connection, mutual support, and empathy is essential for emotional health and happiness. It is like creating a support network in the city, with people who welcome us, inspire us, and help us face challenges.

Finding purpose and meaning: In a constantly transforming world, finding a life purpose or a mission that motivates and gives us direction is fundamental to cultivating hope, optimism, and resilience. It is like having a clear destination in mind—a place that inspires you to move forward and overcome obstacles.

Developing adaptability: The modern world is a constantly changing environment that demands flexibility, creativity, and adaptability. Learning to cope with changes, embrace the new, and reinvent oneself in the face of challenges is essential for navigating future uncertainties with greater confidence and serenity. It is like being an urban explorer, boldly charting new territories in the metropolis with curiosity and courage.

Caring for mental health: Prioritizing mental health is fundamental for facing modern challenges with balance and well-being. Cultivating healthy habits, such as regular physical activity, mindful eating, restorative sleep, and connecting with nature, is like building a sanctuary of peace and tranquility amid the chaos of the city.

The art of emotional management: Emotional management in the modern world is an essential art for maintaining balance in a scenario filled with stimuli, demands, and rapid changes. This skill invites us to slow down, cultivate awareness of our feelings, and find tools to navigate the complexity of the present with serenity and purpose.

By applying practices such as mindfulness, self-care, and prioritizing authentic human connections, we build an internal refuge capable of shielding us from the overload of daily life. In this space of balance, we can make more conscious decisions, preserve our emotional health, and find meaning in every challenge we face.

Thus, even amidst the frenetic rhythm of contemporary life, emotional management allows us to chart a more harmonious and meaningful path. With it, we transform the adversities of the modern world into opportunities for growth and learning, strengthening our ability to live with presence, purpose, and well-being.

Chapter 51
Emotional Management in Practice

Emotional management is not just a theoretical concept or a skill to be used in specific moments; it is a practice that manifests itself in every decision, interaction, and challenge faced daily. Just as an artisan uses their tools to create something unique and beautiful, integrating the tools of emotional management into everyday life is essential to building a more balanced and meaningful life. This practical approach transforms theory into action and allows each choice to reflect intentionality and self-awareness.

Incorporating emotional management into everyday life begins with mindful attention to the present and the impact of emotions on our attitudes and relationships. Recognizing emotional patterns and using them as guides for conscious adjustments is fundamental to maintaining balance even in adverse situations. From organizing routines to managing conflicts, applying assertive communication, empathy, and emotional regulation allows us to transform everyday interactions into opportunities for growth and genuine connection.

This continuous practice also involves cultivating positive emotions and developing resilience in the face of difficulties. Whether by adopting gratitude as a way of seeing life with more clarity and purpose, or by facing challenges as learning opportunities, emotional management offers a solid foundation for personal fulfillment. Integrating these tools into everyday life is more than a choice; it is a commitment to living consciously, promoting well-being for oneself and those around us.

Emotional management is not just about abstract concepts and isolated exercises. It is a continuous practice, a lifestyle that manifests itself in every choice, in every relationship, in every challenge. It is like a gardener who cares for their garden with dedication and love, pruning weeds, watering flowers, and cultivating fertile ground for the blossoming of life.

Applying emotional management in everyday life:

Conscious routine: Start the day with a mindfulness practice, such as meditation or conscious breathing, to calm the mind and connect with the present. Throughout the day, pay attention to your emotions, your thoughts, and your reactions. Observe the triggers that trigger negative emotions and seek to use the emotional regulation tools you have learned.

Healthy relationships: Apply the principles of assertive communication, empathy, and compassion in your relationships with family, friends, co-workers, and romantic partners. Communicate your needs and opinions clearly and respectfully, seek to understand the other person's point of view, and cultivate bonds of affection and trust.

Managing stress: Use relaxation techniques, time management, and problem-solving to deal with the stress of everyday life. Set priorities, delegate tasks, set limits, and set aside time for leisure and rest.

Cultivating positive emotions: Practice gratitude, forgiveness, self-compassion, and positive thinking to nurture your emotional health and cultivate happiness. Focus on the blessings in life, the people you love, positive experiences, and your qualities and achievements.

Overcoming challenges: Use resilience, self-confidence, and persistence to overcome the challenges and adversities that life throws your way. Remember that obstacles are opportunities for learning and growth, and that you have the inner strength to overcome them.

Seeking self-knowledge: Continue to explore your inner world, your thoughts, emotions, values, and beliefs. Invest in your self-knowledge through reading, reflection, meditation, therapy, or other practices that allow you to know yourself more deeply.

Learning from experience: Every day, every interaction, every challenge, you have the opportunity to learn and grow. Be open to new experiences, new knowledge, and new perspectives. Life is a constant school, and every moment is an opportunity to learn and evolve.

Emotional management in practice is a journey of self-discovery and transformation, where each moment of the day becomes an opportunity to cultivate balance, resilience, and well-being. Incorporating it into your routine means acting with intention and awareness, using tools such as mindfulness, assertive communication, and resilience to face challenges and nurture meaningful relationships.

Small habits, such as starting the day with a moment of silence or gratitude, can redefine the way we see the world. Applying empathy in interactions and seeing obstacles as opportunities for growth are fundamental steps to living in a more connected and balanced way.

By practicing emotional management daily, we transform our perspective and strengthen our ability to deal with the complexities of life. This ongoing commitment allows us to flourish as individuals and inspire others around us, creating a positive impact that extends far beyond ourselves.

Chapter 52
Creating an Action Plan

Developing an action plan for emotional management is like drawing up the blueprint for a carefully planned construction, where every detail contributes to creating an environment of balance and growth. This practical approach allows us to transform intentions into concrete actions, guiding each step towards a fuller and more conscious life. An effective plan begins with the clear definition of personal goals, which will serve as the foundation for the entire structure, providing direction and purpose to the journey of self-development.

The first step is to assess the terrain: an honest examination of your current emotions, skills, and challenges. Identifying strengths and areas that need improvement is critical to selecting the most appropriate tools. Each technique chosen, whether it be mindfulness practice, physical exercise, or assertive communication strategies, should align with your goals and lifestyle, forming the basis for consistent and sustainable habits.

Implementing the plan requires continuous monitoring and flexibility for adjustments along the way. Reviewing progress, recognizing achievements, and recalibrating strategies are indispensable steps to maintain motivation and ensure success. By celebrating each step forward, you reinforce your dedication and build, brick by brick, an "inner house" that reflects balance, well-being, and emotional resilience. Thus, your action plan becomes not just a guide, but a reflection of your commitment to a more harmonious and meaningful life.

An action plan is a personalized guide that helps you put into practice the knowledge you have acquired about emotional management. It serves as a map for your journey of self-knowledge and transformation, guiding your choices, motivating your actions, and celebrating your achievements.

Building your inner house:

Goal setting: Start by defining your goals clearly and specifically. What do you want to achieve with emotional management? What aspects of your life do you want to improve? What skills do you want to develop? It's like defining the type of house you want to build, the number of rooms, the architectural style, the features that are important to you.

Self-assessment: Conduct an honest and complete self-assessment of your emotional management skills. What are your strengths? What are your weaknesses? What are the main challenges you face in relation to your emotions? It is like assessing the land where the house will be built, identifying the characteristics of the soil, the slope of the land, the obstacles to be overcome.

Choosing the tools: Based on your goals and your self-assessment, select the emotional management tools that are most appropriate for you. Which relaxation techniques do you prefer? Which mindfulness practices appeal to you? What communication skills do you need to develop? It's like choosing the building materials, tools, and equipment that will be used in the work.

Creating habits: Incorporate the chosen tools into your daily routine, creating healthy habits that promote emotional balance. Set times for practicing meditation, mindful breathing, physical exercise, reading, or any other activity that helps you cultivate well-being. It is like building the habits of taking care of your home, cleaning, organizing, doing preventive maintenance to ensure its durability and comfort.

Monitoring and evaluation: Monitor your progress regularly, evaluating whether the tools and habits you have chosen are helping you achieve your goals. Be open to adjusting your action plan whenever necessary, adapting it to your needs and your progress. It's like following the construction of your house, making the necessary adaptations during the construction process to ensure that the final result is what you want.

Celebrating achievements: Recognize and celebrate every step taken, every goal achieved, every habit incorporated. Celebration is a way to motivate yourself to continue the journey and to acknowledge your efforts and progress. It is like celebrating the completion of your house, throwing a housewarming party to celebrate the achievement and share the joy with loved ones.

Creating an action plan for emotional management is a commitment to personal transformation that empowers us to live with more awareness, balance, and purpose. This construction requires self-knowledge and dedication, but it also offers the opportunity to create a solid foundation for emotional well-being and resilience.

By integrating practical tools into your routine and monitoring your progress regularly, you turn intentions into tangible results. Each adjustment along the way reflects your ability to adapt and strengthens your journey. Recognizing and celebrating achievements, however small, is essential to maintaining motivation and reinforcing your confidence.

This plan is not just a guide, but a reflection of your commitment to a fuller life. Brick by brick, you build an inner space of serenity and strength, where emotional balance becomes a living and lasting practice. This inner house will be your refuge, your foundation, and your most authentic expression of who you are.

Chapter 53
Expanding your Emotional Management Toolkit

Expanding your set of tools for emotional management is like adding new instruments to the repertoire of an experienced craftsman, allowing him to create with even more precision, depth, and versatility. As we explore new techniques and resources, we expand our ability to deal with emotional challenges and nurture a richer and more conscious approach to our well-being. This expansion not only diversifies the possibilities but also personalizes emotional care to meet our unique needs.

The foundation of this process is curiosity and experimentation. Books, articles, and educational resources offer windows to new ideas and approaches, connecting us to different and inspiring perspectives. Technologies such as apps and digital platforms can be valuable allies, making practical and accessible tools available, such as guided meditations and interactive journals. At the same time, courses, workshops, and support groups put us in contact with other people on similar journeys, creating a space for mutual learning and enriching exchange.

It is important to remember that emotional management is a continuous and adaptive journey. Traditional or complementary therapies, such as yoga, meditation, and artistic practices, can be integrated to deepen the connection with our inner selves. At the same time, the simplicity of moments in nature or creative expression in various arts contribute to a fuller balance. With each resource explored, you not only build a more robust emotional management kit, but also refine your ability to cultivate resilience, balance, and fulfillment in every aspect of life.

Just as a craftsman chooses the most appropriate tools for each stage of his creation, you can also select the resources that best suit your needs and your goals. Experiment, explore, discover new ways to nurture your emotional health and build a fuller and more meaningful life.

Expanding your arsenal of well-being:

Books and articles: Reading is an inexhaustible source of knowledge and inspiration. Explore books and articles on emotional management, positive psychology, mindfulness, neuroscience, spirituality, and other topics that interest you. Reading can offer you new perspectives, expand your horizons, and introduce you to new tools and techniques.

Apps and digital platforms: Technology can be a powerful ally in emotional management. There are several apps and digital platforms that offer guided meditations, breathing exercises, personal development programs, gratitude journals, and other tools for cultivating well-being.

Courses and workshops: Participating in courses and workshops on emotional management can provide you with a more immersive and interactive learning experience. In these spaces, you can share experiences with other people, learn from qualified instructors, and delve deeper into specific topics.

Support groups: Sharing experiences and connecting with people facing similar challenges can be a source of support, inspiration, and motivation. Look for support groups in your community or online where you can feel comfortable sharing your feelings, receiving and offering support, and learning from the experiences of others.

Therapy and professional support: Therapy is a safe and confidential space to explore emotional, behavioral, and relationship issues with the help of a qualified professional. A therapist can help you identify dysfunctional behavior patterns, develop emotional management skills, and build a healthier, more balanced life.

Complementary practices: Explore complementary practices that promote physical, mental, and emotional well-being, such as yoga, meditation, acupuncture, massage, aromatherapy, and other integrative therapies.

Contact with nature: Nature is an inexhaustible source of peace, beauty, and renewal. Take time to connect with nature, whether it's walking in a park, watching the sea, tending a garden, or simply contemplating the beauty of the starry sky.

Artistic expression: Art is a powerful form of emotional expression, creativity, and self-knowledge. Explore different forms of artistic expression, such as painting, music, dance, writing, theater, and discover new ways to connect with your emotions and give vent to your creativity.

Expanding your emotional management toolkit is an opportunity to enrich your journey with new tools, techniques, and practices that resonate with your essence. Each resource explored becomes an ally in building a more balanced, connected, and meaningful life, helping you to face emotional challenges with greater versatility and confidence.

As we experience new paths - whether through reading, technology, art or nature - we discover deeper layers of self-awareness and well-being. This expansion invites us to integrate diverse knowledge, creating a unique emotional arsenal that reflects our individuality and connects us to a wider network of human experiences.

With curiosity and openness, each tool added to your kit transforms your emotional management practice into a living art. This continuous evolution not only strengthens your resilience, but also opens doors to new forms of expression, learning, and connection with the world around you.

Chapter 54
Maintaining Balance

Emotional management is like a marathon that requires preparation, discipline, and consistency. To maintain emotional balance in the long term, it is essential to establish consistent habits that serve as the foundation for a calmer and healthier life. Just as a long-distance runner adjusts their pace to avoid exhaustion, we also need to find a suitable rhythm to take care of our body, mind, and emotions, maintaining consistency even amidst challenges.

Emotional balance is sustained by simple and effective practices. Setting aside time for meditation or mindful breathing, adopting a balanced diet, and prioritizing sleep are fundamental pillars. These practices not only strengthen the ability to deal with daily stress but also create a solid foundation for resilience. In addition, recognizing and celebrating small achievements on the path of emotional management are ways to reinforce motivation and cultivate optimism, ensuring renewed energy to continue the journey.

The key to maintaining balance lies in remaining flexible and adaptable. Just as a marathon runner adjusts their strategy depending on the course conditions, we need to adjust to life's changes. Flexibility allows us to overcome obstacles, redefine goals, and continue with lightness. By cultivating this dynamic and conscious approach, we build a stable foundation for an emotionally balanced life, full of purpose and satisfaction.

Just as a marathon runner prepares for the race with regular training, proper nutrition, and sufficient rest, we also need to cultivate habits that help us maintain emotional balance throughout life. These habits are like fuel for our journey, giving us energy, endurance, and vitality to face challenges and move forward with lightness and determination.

Running the marathon of life:

Pace and consistency: Just as a marathon runner maintains a constant pace to avoid exhaustion before the end of the race, in emotional management it is also important to cultivate consistency and discipline. Practice meditation, mindful breathing, physical exercise, and other healthy habits regularly, even when you feel unmotivated or short on time. Consistency is key to building a solid foundation of well-being and resilience.

Hydration and nutrition: Just as a marathon runner hydrates and nourishes themselves properly during the race, in emotional management it is also essential to nourish the body and mind with healthy food, water, and good thoughts. A balanced diet, rich in fruits, vegetables, provides essential nutrients for the proper functioning of the body and brain. Cultivating positive thoughts, practicing gratitude, and connecting with loved ones nourishes the soul and strengthens the spirit.

Rest and recovery: Just as a marathon runner needs rest to recover energy and prevent injuries, in emotional management, it is also essential to prioritize sleep, relaxation, and moments of peace and quiet. Restorative sleep allows the body and mind to regenerate, and moments of relaxation help reduce stress and anxiety.

Overcoming obstacles: Just as a marathon runner faces climbs, descents, and other obstacles along the way, in life we also encounter challenges and difficulties that test our resilience and determination. Using the tools of emotional management, such as resilience, persistence, and optimism, helps us overcome these obstacles and move forward with more strength and confidence.

Focus on the goal: Just as a marathon runner keeps their focus on the finish line, in emotional management it is important to keep your focus on your goals and motivations. Remember your dreams, your values, and the benefits that a balanced and happy life can bring you. Focus keeps us motivated and gives us the strength to continue the journey.

Adaptation and flexibility: Just as a marathon runner needs to adapt to weather conditions, terrain, and unforeseen events that may arise during the race, in emotional management it is also important to be flexible and adapt to changes and challenges that life throws our way. Flexibility allows us to adjust our pace, change strategy, and move forward with more lightness and efficiency.

Celebration and gratitude: Just as a marathon runner celebrates the achievement of reaching the finish line, in emotional management it is important to celebrate each stage overcome, each habit incorporated, each lesson learned. Gratitude for small victories and progress made fills us with joy, motivation, and energy to continue the journey.

Maintaining emotional balance is an ongoing commitment, similar to a marathon where each step strengthens our resilience and brings us closer to a fuller and more satisfying life. Consistent daily practices, such as taking care of the body, nourishing the mind, and cultivating positive emotions, form the foundation of this journey. Flexibility is essential to adjust the pace in the face of unforeseen events, allowing us to move forward with lightness and confidence. Recognizing that challenges are part of the journey helps us to see them as opportunities for learning and growth, reinforcing our determination. Celebrating each achievement, no matter how small, connects us to the purpose of the journey and renews our energy to move forward. With a constant rhythm, adaptation, and gratitude, we build lasting emotional balance, which sustains us in all stages of the marathon of life.

Chapter 55
Reaping the Fruits of Emotional Management

The journey through the universe of emotional management is a journey of self-knowledge and transformation that rewards us with valuable fruits. Healthier relationships, greater resilience in the face of challenges, lasting inner peace, and a renewed purpose are just some of the treasures gained by mastering the art of managing emotions. Just like a farmer who dedicates time and patience to cultivating their land, we will reap the benefits of constant care for our emotional health.

As we move forward on this journey, we realize that it does not have an end point, but rather a continuous flow of learning and growth. Emotional management is a daily commitment, a dynamic process of adjustment and evolution. It is like taking care of a garden: by pruning what no longer serves, watering regularly, and paying attention to the needs of flowers and plants, we ensure that the environment flourishes in harmony and beauty.

May the tools and lessons learned along this path continue to guide every decision, every relationship, and every challenge that arises. Remember that the map of this journey is in your hands, and the choices you make today will define the future you want to build. With dedication and confidence in your ability to learn and grow, emotional management will be an essential ally in your life journey, helping you to create a more conscious, balanced, and meaningful path.

Just like a farmer who cultivates the land with dedication and patience, reaping the fruits of their labor throughout the seasons, we too can reap the fruits of emotional management in our daily lives. Healthier relationships, greater resilience in the face of challenges, physical and mental well-being, inner peace, self-knowledge, happiness, and purpose - these are some of the treasures we can find by mastering the art of navigating emotions.

Emotional management is not a destination, but rather a continuous journey of learning and growth. It is a commitment to oneself, a constant search for balance, awareness, and inner harmony. It is like a garden that needs to be cultivated with love, dedication, and attention so that the flowers of happiness, peace, and personal fulfillment can flourish in all their fullness.

May this journey through the world of emotional management be just the beginning of a more conscious, balanced, and happy life. May the tools and knowledge acquired along this path accompany you in every step, in every choice, in every relationship, in every challenge. And may you reap the fruits of emotional management in all aspects of your life, building a more promising, meaningful, and fulfilling future.

Emotional management is a legacy that we leave to ourselves, a journey of care and transformation that flourishes in every aspect of our existence. The fruits harvested - deeper relationships, greater balance, resilience, and an authentic connection with our purpose - remind us of the power of our choices and the impact of self-knowledge on our lives. By continuing to cultivate this inner garden with patience and attention, we ensure that it thrives in all seasons. Each practice adopted, each reflection incorporated, and each emotion welcomed are seeds planted for a fuller and more meaningful future. This is a never-ending process, where constant learning strengthens our path and renews our strength.

May these fruits be celebrated and shared, nourishing not only your growth but also inspiring those around you. With dedication, emotional management not only transforms your journey but also illuminates the world, proving that inner balance is the foundation for a truly fulfilling life.

Epilogue

Dear reader,

As I finish this book, I feel a deep gratitude for having walked this path by your side. It is with humility and joy that I bid farewell to these pages, hoping that they have echoed in your heart and opened new horizons on your personal journey.

Writing this book was, for me, a transformative experience. Each word, each concept, each shared reflection was born from a deep desire to contribute to the construction of a more conscious, compassionate, and emotionally intelligent world.

Throughout these chapters, we explored together the fascinating universe of emotions. We investigated the secret language they speak, their complex mechanisms, their nuances, and their paradoxes. We delved into the depths of the human psyche, unraveling the mysteries of the mind and the paths that lead to self-knowledge, healing, and personal transformation.

I hope this book has been more than just a read. May it have been a dialogue between us, an invitation to reflection, a provocation for you to reconnect with your inner wisdom and awaken the master that resides within you.

Thank you for joining me on this journey. I hope the tools and knowledge shared here will help you to walk your path with more clarity, confidence, and serenity. May this book be a guide for your journey of self-knowledge, healing, and personal transformation.

Remember: emotions are like compasses that guide us through the paths of life. By learning to listen to them with attention and respect, we can navigate the waters of existence more safely, transforming challenges into opportunities and building a fuller, more authentic, and meaningful life.

With gratitude,
Amadeu Rossi

www.ingramcontent.com/pod-product-compliance
Lightning Source LLC
LaVergne TN
LVHW040049080526
838202LV00045B/3552